"NEW STUDIES EXPLAIN
PROTECTIVE BENEFITS OF MOTHER'S MILK.

"Scientists studying the chemistry of breast milk are finding that it is uniquely constituted to foster the health and growth of the human infant. . . Breastfed babies are healthier than those raised on bottled formulas.

"Researchers have found that mother's milk harbors an arsenal of immunological weapons believed to protect the baby against infections and allergies for months until the baby's own defenses are more fully developed. Such weapons are lacking in cow's milk.

"Other chemicals recently found in human breast milk are thought to stimulate the development of organs such as the intestinal tract and possibly the brain.

"Remarked Dr. W. Allan Walker of Massachusetts General Hospital, a leading researcher in the field, 'We'll discover a lot more factors in breast milk that enhance its protective and nutritive value.' "

—*THE NEW YORK TIMES*

THE COMPLETE BOOK OF BREASTFEEDING

"The Gospel . . . Comprehensive, easy reading, clearly written!"

—Benjamin Segal, M.D., F.A.C.S.

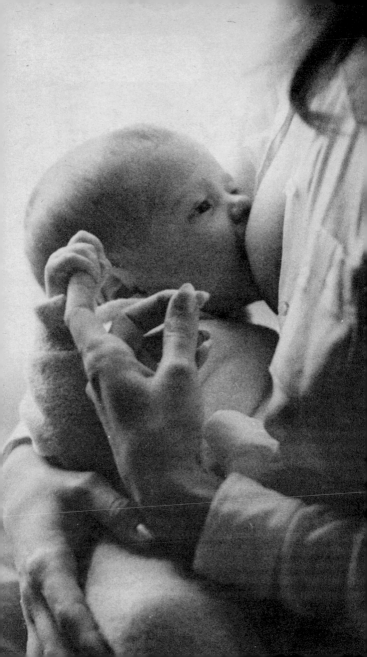

The Complete Book of Breastfeeding

by Marvin S. Eiger, M.D. and
Sally Wendkos Olds

Photographs by Kathryn Abbe
Line Art by Norma Erler Rahn

BANTAM BOOKS
TORONTO · NEW YORK · LONDON · SYDNEY · AUCKLAND

THE COMPLETE BOOK OF BREASTFEEDING

A Bantam Book published by arrangement with
Workman Publishing Co., Inc.

PRINTING HISTORY

Workman edition published April 1972

Bantam edition / September 1972

2nd printing . . . . . January 1974	9th printing . . . . July 1977
3rd printing . . . . June 1974	10th printing . . . . May 1978
4th printing . . . . February 1975	11th printing . . November 1978
5th printing . . . . . . August 1976	12th printing . . . . . . June 1979
6th printing . . . . . . August 1976	13th printing . . . . July 1979
7th printing . . . . . January 1977	14th printing . . . February 1980
8th printing . . . . April 1977	15th printing . . . . . August 1980
	16th printing . . . . April 1981

Cover photographs courtesy of Erika Stone
Text Photographs by Kathryn Abbe
Line art by Norma Erler Rahn

ISBN 0-553-20224-3

Published simultaneously in the United States and Canada

---

*Bantam Books are published by Bantam Books, Inc. Its trade-
mark, consisting of the words "Bantam Books" and the por-
trayal of a bantam, is Registered in U.S. Patent and Trademark
Office and in other countries. Marca Registrada. Bantam
Books, Inc., 666 Fifth Avenue, New York, New York 10103.*

ACKNOWLEDGMENTS

We want to express our grateful appreciation to the many friends and colleagues who generously gave of their expertise and time, who contributed the fruits of their research and experience and offered valuable suggestions to aid us in making this book as helpful as possible to nursing mothers.

Our heartfelt thanks go to Harry Bakwin, M.D., Saul Blatman, M.D., Samuel Stone, M.D., T. Berry Brazelton, M.D., Michael J. Brennan, M.D., Nathaniel S. Cooper, D.D.S., Mary Cossman, Lois Dwyer, Paul Elber, Sylvia Feldman, Ph.D., Samuel J. Fomon, M.D., Florence Fralin, Vincent Freda, M.D., Lawrence M. Gartner, M.D., Barbara Goodheart, Elizabeth Hormann, Derrick B. Jelliffe, M.D., Tobe Joffe, Alice Ladas, Ed.P., Philip Lipsitz, M.D., Michael Newton, M.D., Niles Newton, Ph.D., Kathleen O'Regan, R.N., Alice Rossi, Ph.D., Asoka Roy, R.N., C.N.M., M.S., Benjamin Segal, M.D., Evelyn B. Thoman, Ph.D., Marian Tompson, Tilla Vahanian, Ed.D., the staffs of the Departments of Pediatrics at Beth Israel Hospital Medical Center and New York University Medical Center and of the Newborn Service at University Hospital and, of course, to the many nursing mothers who shared with us their thoughts and feelings about breastfeeding.

We received valuable information and help from the following organizations: The American Academy of Pediatrics, The American College of Obstetricians and Gynecologists, The American Medical Association, The American Dental Association, La Leche League International, The American Cancer Society, The International Childbirth Education Association, The National Institute of Child Health and Human Development, and The New York Academy of Medicine.

And, finally, we want to express our love and appreciation of our own families—Mark, Nancy, Jenny, and Dora Olds; and Phyllis, Michael, and Pamela Eiger—for their constant encouragement and support.

CONTENTS

INTRODUCTION

If you were living at some other time or in some other place, you might not need this book. You might even wonder about its purpose, since you would be getting much of the information in these pages from your mother, your aunts, your older sisters, and your neighbors. They would share with you their breastfeeding experiences and those of their mothers before them. As you saw them suckling their infants, you would pick up the "tricks of the trade" without even realizing it. It would never occur to you that you would not nurse your baby, because every baby that you had ever seen would have been fed at his mother's breast—except in the extremely rare case when a mother was too ill to nurse.

But today in our western world, you may easily reach adulthood without ever having seen a mother nursing her baby. You may want to breastfeed, but have many questions that neither your mother nor your friends can answer accurately. Even the physicians who give you such good advice on other aspects of your own and your baby's well-being may know very little about the art of breastfeeding.

Dr. Alice K. Ladas, a New York psychologist, recently set out to discover to what extent information and support were related to successful breastfeeding. "Is the modern American woman really less capable than her forebears of suckling her young?" Dr. Ladas wondered. "Or is she simply not receiving the proper kind of encouragement and help?" By studying the breastfeeding histories of 756 women, Dr. Ladas found that the reasons given by every woman in the group who had stopped breastfeeding her first child sooner than she would have liked to do so were related to lack of information about breastfeeding. Dr. Ladas also found that the degree of encouragement exhibited by husbands, physicians, friends, and relatives was an important factor of success.

With this book, then, we two authors—one, a pediatrician

who has learned much of what he knows about breastfeeding from the successful nursing mothers of his young patients and the other, a medical writer who nursed her own three children—hope to provide you with the practical information you need.

We want to share the most up-to-date knowledge and the most helpful techniques of this feminine art with expectant mothers who plan to breastfeed their infants, mothers who are already nursing their babies and readers who simply wonder about the place of breastfeeding in this modern age. We want to assure you that, as a healthy, well-informed mother, you should have every expectation of being able to nurse your baby for as long as you and he* both want to be part of what a British psychiatrist has termed the "nursing couple."

Breastfeeding is easy; there is nothing complicated about it. Yet it is a paradox and a puzzle that in a well-developed, medically advanced country like ours, only 25% of all women even begin to breastfeed their babies and as many as 62% of those women give it up after a brief trial. Many reasons have been offered for this seeming inability of healthy, well-nourished civilized women to nurse their babies. Probably the two most important ones are the expectation of failure and the easy availability of alternatives. If a mother in a more primitive country fails to nurse her baby successfully, the baby will probably have to be turned over to another nursing

---

*Throughout this book, we will always use the masculine pronoun to refer to your baby. This is not because either of us is prejudiced against baby girls; both of us have daughters of our own and value them highly as individuals. It is simply because we wish to avoid the constant repetition of "he or she," "him or her," "his or hers." Our language has a great need for pronouns that are equally applicable to males and females. As of this writing, however, we feel we can communicate most easily by using the limited words we already have. You are most definitely a "she"; for simplicity, in this book, your baby will always be a "he."

woman. If an American woman decides that she will not or cannot breastfeed, she has only to go to the corner drugstore for an adequate supply of food. Furthermore, in most countries, women expect as a matter of course that they will breastfeed their babies. In our country, the average woman has little or no confidence that she will be able to feed her baby this natural way. The woman who does become a successful nursing mother often succeeds in spite of her family and friends' expectations of her failure.

Another reason for failure in breastfeeding is simple ignorance of techniques. Nursing a baby may fulfill an instinctive drive, but the actual breastfeeding procedures constitute an art that must be learned. Some mothers breastfeed their babies by "just doing what comes naturally," puzzled by no questions and troubled by no problems. Most new mothers, however, do have questions about all aspects of infant care and seem to have the most trouble finding authoritative answers to their questions about breastfeeding. Sometimes, the lack of information makes them hesitate to embark upon an adventure that seems strange and bewildering. Other times, they reluctantly switch to the bottle when, had their questions been answered and their problems solved, they would have much preferred to continue being part of a nursing couple.

There are three essential tools for successful breastfeeding: the knowledge of what to do, the confidence that you are doing the right thing for your baby and yourself, and the determination to persist in the face of any minor setbacks that may come your way. We hope that this little book will help you develop all three.

Marvin S. Eiger, M.D.
Sally Wendkos Olds

CHAPTER 1.

SHOULD YOU OR SHOULDN'T YOU?

Only in relatively recent times has there been any question at all as to whether a mother would breastfeed her baby. With the advent of dependable refrigeration and pasteurization, however, there is now a choice. You can decide whether you want to feed your baby the way mothers have done from time immemorial—or whether you want to take advantage of modern technology and provide your baby's nourishment in a bottle.

Many factors will enter into your decision—the customs of your community, the attitudes of your obstetrician, your pediatrician, your husband, your style of life, your personality, and your feelings about mothering. In some countries, it is taken for granted that a woman will breastfeed her children. Some governments, such as that in Switzerland, where the picture of a nursing mother appears on the fifty-franc note, actively encourage breastfeeding by paying nursing mothers.

In the United States, the nursing mother is the nonconformist, a member of a minority group. It seems, however, that the long-term trend away from breastfeeding is now being reversed, at least among better-educated, middle- and upper-class women. Since these women led the movement away from breastfeeding in generations past, perhaps their renewed interest will spur a similar resurgence in the country at large.

Before you decide how you will feed your baby, you will want to consider the advantages of breastfeeding for both baby and mother, and its ramifications in your personal situation.

BENEFITS FOR THE BABY

HEALTH

From the physiological point of view, the breast is best. Recent studies do not show significant differences in rates of illness between breastfed and bottle-fed infants of middle- or upper-class parents in well-developed countries. However, among parents who are less medically sophisticated and in hot climates with less than optimal sanitary conditions, the picture changes radically. In tropical countries, the breastfed baby may have six times the chance for life as his bottle-fed cousin.

Breast milk can never be contaminated by the harmful bacteria that may multiply in standing animal milk; it is always served to the baby in a clean container. It cannot be over-diluted to save money. Mistakes cannot be made in its preparation.

There may be other reasons, too, why breast milk is healthier. Some medical researchers feel that specific antibodies against disease germs reach the infant through his mother's milk, while others attribute its immunological benefits to the action of "unspecific factors of unknown origin." There is also some speculation that breast milk contains no antibodies of its own, but is able to stimulate antibody production in the baby's system. There are definite indications that babies are protected from influenza, from polio, and from diarrhea by substances in their mothers' milk.

In highly developed countries such as ours, where sanitary conditions are generally good, the gap in health between the breastfed and the bottle-fed baby is narrowed considerably. In addition, modern antibiotic medicines can now vanquish many of the illnesses that used to be fatal to infants. Preventing an infection, however, is still better than curing it. And there *is* some basis for belief that breast milk does, indeed, have certain preventive, protective powers.

DIGESTIBILITY

A baby can digest human milk more easily than he can digest the milk of other animals. Breast milk forms softer curds in the infant's stomach than cow's milk, and is more quickly assimilated into his system. While it contains less protein than does cow's milk, virtually all the protein in breast milk is used by the baby, whereas about half the protein in cow's milk is wasted, passing through his body and making extra work for his excretory system.

The breastfed baby is less apt to get diarrhea than the bottle-fed baby—and he can never become constipated, since breast milk cannot solidify in his intestinal tract to form hard stools. While he may soil every diaper in his early days or go several days without a bowel movement later on, neither of these situations will indicate intestinal upset.

Some premature infants and other babies with sensitive digestive systems are known to thrive only on breast milk. If their own mothers do not provide it, they must obtain it from other mothers.

ALLERGY

While most babies do well on either breast or formula, an occasional infant seems to be allergic to the formula he first receives. When such a baby suffers indigestion or diarrhea, the hunt is on to find a formula that will not upset the baby. The mother faced with this problem may feel like a chemist in the lab as, on the advice of her pediatrician, she tries different proportions and different kinds of milks and sugars, even going occasionally to such exotica as goat's milk or soybean milk.

The breastfeeding mother never has this concern, since no baby is allergic to breast milk. An occasional infant may, however, develop an allergic reaction such as vomiting, diarrhea, skin rash, hives, or sniffles, to some substance in his mother's diet that is transmitted through the milk. With a little trial and error, it is usually possible for the mother to identify the allergenic food and stop eating it as long as she continues to nurse.

Another rare condition, not precisely an allergy but a reaction by the infant to a substance in the mother's milk, is breast-milk jaundice, discussed in Chapter Nine. Occasionally, a baby who develops this generally harmless condition has to be taken off the breast temporarily but can resume normal breastfeeding after only a few days.

Neither of these situations is a true allergic reaction to the breast milk itself. In fact, there are indications that breast milk may even prevent allergies. In one classic study of more than 20,000 infants, those who were fed artificially were seven times as likely to get eczema (a skin disorder associated with allergy) as those who were completely breastfed. If you or your husband is particularly allergy-prone, you have a special reason for nursing your baby.

HUMAN MILK FOR HUMAN BABIES

Chemical analysis has shown that the milk of every species is different in its composition from every other milk. We can logically assume from this that each animal produces in its milk those elements most important for the survival of its young. While artificial formula can closely imitate mother's milk, it can never duplicate it exactly. No manufacturer has ever claimed that his formula product is just as good as or better than breast milk, and it is highly doubtful that such an audacious claim will ever be made. About fifteen years ago, leading infant formulas were found to be deficient in a substance called pyroxidine; only a couple of years ago, the amount of folic acid in baby formula was deemed insufficient. Who knows what other ingredients will be isolated and identified in mother's milk for the formula-makers to attempt to imitate?

The breastfed baby differs in so many respects from his bottle-fed counterpart that one pediatrician, Dr. Harry Bakwin, has said that he is practically a different animal. The ratio of vitamins in his system is different, as is the composition of various substances in his blood. In addition, the bacteria in his intestinal tract are strikingly different. While all human beings harbor a large and varied population of intestinal bacteria, a single innocuous species, *Lactobacillus bifidus,* makes up more than 90% and sometimes more than 99% of the total bacteria found in the feces of a nursing infant. *L. bifidus* is also present in the stool of the bottle-fed baby, but only as one of a crowd of many other species. It is possible that this harmless organism is the only intestinal microbe that can survive the highly acid environment of the nursling's intestinal tract.

The breastfed baby even grows differently from the bottle baby, who develops bigger and heavier bones during his first year of life—probably due to the larger amounts of calcium in cow's milk. Some people feel that breastfed babies are deficient in calcium, but it seems more likely that the formula-fed baby is exhibiting an artificial growth pattern—much like the force-fed Strasbourg geese.

Even though we don't know the precise reasons for, or the significance of, all the differences between the baby nourished at the breast and the baby fed by bottle, it seems logical to assume that the best first food for your baby is the one served up by Mother Nature.

THE NATURAL WAY

At a time when so much of our life has an unsettlingly unnatural aspect—with chemicals in the air we breathe, the clothes we wear, and the foods we eat—more and more of us are striving to recapture some of the natural joys of life on earth. When you breastfeed your baby, you know that you are giving him the natural food intended just for him. Its purity is tainted by no synthetic compounds, no preservatives, no artificial ingredients. Breast milk is the ultimate health food.

If you are concerned about the environment your baby will grow up in, we think you will agree that the breast is also best from the ecological point of view. Feeding the bottle-fed baby entails the use and disposal of dozens of cans of formula, the cardboard cartons in which they are packaged, and the baby's

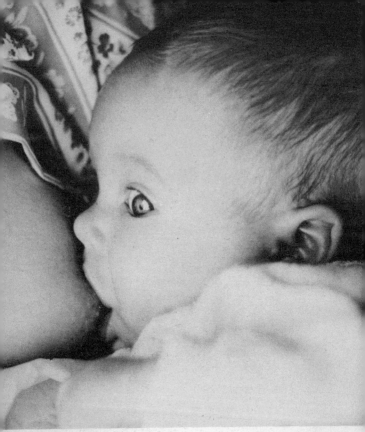

bottles and nipples which are also discarded either after one use, as in the case of disposable bottles, or after a few months use. To wash the baby's feeding utensils, soap or detergents, water, and the energy used to heat the water must all be expended.

TOOTH AND JAW DEVELOPMENT

Apart from the nutritional benefits of breast milk, suckling at the breast is good for your baby's tooth and jaw development. The infant at the breast has to use as much as sixty times more energy to get his food than does the baby drinking from a bottle. The nursling has to mouth the entire areola (the brown area surrounding the nipple), move his jaws back and forth, and squeeze hard with his gums to extract the milk. To accomplish this arduous task, your baby has been endowed with jaw muscles relatively three times stronger than those of his mother or father. As these muscles are strenuously exercised in suckling, their constant pulling encourages well-formed jaws and straight, healthy teeth.

One factor accounting for many dental malformations that eventually send youngsters to the orthodontist or the speech therapist is an abnormal swallowing pattern, known as "tongue thrust." This is very common among bottle-fed babies, but almost nonexistent among the breastfed. To understand why, we have to examine the mechanisms of feeding. The baby at the breast moves his lower jaw back and forth quite vigorously to stimulate the flow of milk. He pushes his tongue upward against the flattened nipple to keep it in his mouth. As the milk begins to come, he sucks it in and swallows. He then repeats the whole process, so that a feeding session involves a constant succession of chewing and suckling motions.

The bottle-fed baby does not have to exercise his jaws so energetically, since light suckling alone produces a rapid flow of milk. In fact, since the milk flows so freely from the bottle, the infant actually has to learn how to protect himself from an over-supply so that he will not choke. He pushes his tongue forward against the nipple holes to stem the flow to a level that he can easily handle. The tongue that should be pressing upward has instead come forward, and a swallowing pattern that will most likely persist throughout the child's life has begun. Many dentists feel that such forward tongue thrust can result in mouth breathing, lip biting, gum disease, and an unattractive appearance.

Of course, not all bottle-fed babies develop dental problems, and some breastfed babies do. In addition, a new type of "orthodontic" nipple, the Nuk Sauger, has been designed to avoid the development of "tongue thrust" and its effects. Despite its much closer approximation to the human nipple, however, there is no doubt that the "real thing" will continue to remain superior to all its imitators.

Besides the development of good swallowing habits, there is another factor that contributes to the breastfed child's healthy tooth and jaw development. Since he gets more of the sucking that most babies seem to need, he is less likely to suck his thumb. The bottle-fed baby must stop sucking the nipple as soon as his bottle is empty, to avoid ingesting air; the baby at the breast can continue in this blissful pastime until either you or he decides he's been at the well long enough.

AVAILABILITY

Another advantage enjoyed by the nursling is the constant availability of milk. His dinner is always ready, always at the right temperature, always the same consistency. He never has to struggle to get milk from a nipple with scanty holes, nor does he have to gulp furiously to keep up with a gush from extra-large holes. No snowstorm, no flood, no car breakdown, no milk-drivers' strike can keep his food from him. As long as mother is near, so is dinner.

EMOTIONAL GRATIFICATION

A great deal has been written and said about the psychological benefits the baby derives from breastfeeding. Dr. Niles Newton, a psychologist who has devoted much of her professional career to studies of lactation in humans and in laboratory animals, has found many psychological differences between breast and artificial feeding, most of which seem to tip the scales in favor of breastfeeding. For example, lactating mice demonstrate a greater drive than non-nursing mice in overcoming obstacles to reach their infants, indicating some mechanism in lactation itself that triggers maternal behavior. Also, such factors as the more intimate interaction between the breastfeeding mother and child and the more immediate satisfaction of the nursing baby's hunger seem, from the psychological point of view, to augur healthier mental development.

However, as important as early feeding experiences may be to a child's later development, there are so many variables in a family relationship that it is impossible to say that breast-feeding *per se* produces a well-adjusted individual. The mother who breastfeeds only because she thinks it is her duty to do so communicates her resentment to her child. The mother who weans suddenly and traumatically can undo much of the good that has been built up in the nursing relationship. The frustration encountered by a hungry baby whose mother does not have enough milk can over-balance the benefits of breastfeeding. Partly for these reasons, it is virtually impossible to say that breastfeeding is always psychologically superior to bottle feeding.

And, while investigators have been conducting studies for the past forty years to try to correlate method of infant feeding with later personality development, none of these studies have proved that either breast- or bottle-feeding—by itself—will guarantee that a baby will become a secure, well-adjusted person.

Psychiatrists and other students of human and animal nature do state categorically, however, that a baby does gain a sense of security from the warmth and closeness of the mother's body. When you breastfeed your baby, you cannot be tempted—even on your busiest days—to lay your baby down in his crib with a propped bottle. You *have* to draw him close to you for every single feeding. While the bottle-feeding mother can also show her love for her baby by holding him and cuddling him at feeding times, in actual practice she tends to do less of this. And, of course, she cannot duplicate the unique skin-to-skin contact between the nursing mother and her infant. Many adults today are going out of their way to join encounter groups, sensitivity groups, T-groups, and other forms of group therapy in settings that encourage a large measure of hugging, hand-holding, and other forms of touching. It is possible that many of those who respond so well in these groups are trying to make up for that close bodily contact they missed as infants.

Babies also gain a sense of well-being from secure handling, and the mother who nurses her baby often seems more confident in her management of him. Whether the woman who is sure of her maternal abilities is more likely to breastfeed—or whether the experience of being a good provider infuses her with self-confidence—is difficult to answer. It does seem that the mother who nurses is more likely to know how to soothe her baby when he is upset—perhaps because the very act of putting him to the breast is such a comfort to him that she does not have to search for other ways of reassuring him. The breast is more than a pipeline for getting food into the baby. It is warmth, it is reassurance, it is comfort.

BENEFITS FOR THE MOTHER

Your primary reason for wanting to breastfeed is probably your awareness that it will be better for your baby. You may not have realized that nursing offers a world of benefits for you, too.

GOOD FOR THE FIGURE

Nursing your baby will help you to regain your figure more quickly, since the process of lactation causes the uterus (which has increased during pregnancy to about twenty times its normal size) to shrink more quickly to its pre-pregnancy size. During the early days of nursing, you can actually feel the uterus contracting while your baby suckles. As he nurses, he stimulates certain nerves in the nipples which bring about the uterine contractions. These contractions hasten uterine involution (return to former size) and the expulsion of excess tissue and blood from the uterus.

CONVENIENCE

Breastfeeding is much easier than preparing formula. When asked why they decided to breastfeed, many women answer, "Because I'm lazy." We live in a world of conveniences, in which each manufacturer tries to outdo the other in providing "less work for the homemaker." In the area of infant feeding, no efficiency expert alive has been able to outdo nature. It's so easy just to wake up in the morning, pick up the baby and put him to the breast. You don't have to mix formula. You don't have to scrub and sterilize bottles and nipples. You don't have to stagger to the kitchen in the middle of the night to heat a bottle. Your baby's daily batch of food prepares itself in its own attractive, permanent containers. You have the pleasure of feeding your baby, with none of the bother. You'll enjoy that extra hour or so you save by not having to sterilize bottles and make formula. And since your breastfed baby won't need solid foods for some two to three months later than the bottle baby, you'll be spared the spoon-feeding routine for a while, too.

When you breastfeed, you never have to make up an extra bottle at the last minute, nor throw out formula that your baby doesn't want. Working on the time-honored principle of supply and demand, your mammary glands produce the amount of milk your baby wants.

You'll find it easier to go visiting or traveling with your baby, since you won't have to take along bottles, nipples and formula, nor will you have to worry about refrigeration and dishwashing facilities.

ECONOMY

Breastfeeding is cheaper. If you have already been maintaining a healthy, well-balanced diet, you need to eat nothing special to provide for the manufacture of milk. The small amounts of extra food that you'll be eating to make up for the calories you lose in the milk will cost you less than you would have to pay for bottles, nipples, sterilizing equipment, and formula. It is ironic that in our country, the women in the lowest income groups, where sanitary conditions are least favorable and finances least plentiful, are also the least likely to take advantage of the practical benefits of breastfeeding.

ESTHETICS

If you have a sensitive nose, you will appreciate the fact that your breastfed baby smells better. Both his bowel movements and the excess milk that he sometimes spits up after a feeding smell mild and inoffensive, unlike the bottle-fed baby's.

YOUR HEALTH

Every mother of an infant needs adequate rest. The many physiological changes of pregnancy, the hard work of labor and delivery, and the demanding care of a new baby all deplete your energy. When you breastfeed, you are forced to relax during your baby's feeding times, since you cannot prop a bottle or turn the baby over to someone else in the family while you run around straightening up the house.

Thromboembolism, a potentially dangerous disorder in which a blood clot breaks loose from its site of formation to block a blood vessel, is a rare complication of childbirth. Women who are over twenty-five, who have had several children, or who have had surgical deliveries have a slightly higher risk of thromboembolism. Two recent British studies found that these higher-risk patients were at even higher risk if lactation was suppressed. This may have been the result of the hormones administered to suppress lactation, or it may have been the result of the suppression itself. In any case, the evidence from these two studies suggests that the hormonal suppression of lactation may tip the scales against those women already predisposed to such clotting disorders.

It is also worth noting that some cancer researchers state that the risk of developing breast cancer is lowest for women who have borne and nursed children. The relationship between breastfeeding and breast cancer is discussed more fully in Chapter Nine.

BIRTH CONTROL

Breastfeeding acts as a natural, albeit unreliable, means of spacing children. While your baby is receiving nothing but breast milk—no solid foods nor any formula at all—you are less likely to become pregnant than the non-nursing or partially nursing mother. This is because the fully lactating woman rarely ovulates. (She rarely menstruates, also, which might be considered another plus.) *Nursing a baby is not a guarantee against pregnancy, however.* While you are less likely to conceive while you are maintaining your baby solely on your milk, it is possible that you might become pregnant. If you want to plan the size and spacing of your family, you should use some form of contraception. (This will be discussed more fully in Chapter Eight.)

ENJOYMENT

Very little attention is usually given to the fact that breastfeeding can be an intensely pleasurable, sensuous act. Suckling a baby gives rise to some of the same physical responses that occur during sexual intercourse, such as the discharge of the hormone *oxytocin,* contractions of the uterus, erection of the nipples, and an elevation of body temperature. Masters and Johnson, the researchers who have contributed so much to our knowledge of physiological sexual response, report in their book, *Human Sexual Response,* that women who nursed their babies were more interested in resuming sexual activity with their husbands than were non-nursing mothers. This may be because the nursing experience itself contains a measure of sexual stimulation—or perhaps because the woman who is more comfortable with her body is more likely to nurse her babies.

FEMININE FULFILLMENT

All these benefits are real. Any one of them might be a valid reason for deciding to breastfeed. Yet the woman who has a choice between breast and bottle and decides to nurse her baby often makes her final decision on a completely different basis—the emotional satisfaction and enormous sense of fulfillment gained from breastfeeding an infant. As one young mother has said, "There is something very right about

a system that makes one human being so happy about being responsible for another. I could never have the same good feeling of accomplishment by relying on the neighborhood store or the dairy for my baby's milk. Knowing that I was giving him something no one else could give him created a tie between us that became one of my deepest joys."

Women who have bottle-fed one baby and nursed another usually say that they felt closer to their nursing infants—even though as the babies grew, this difference did not continue to exist. A common reaction is reflected in this statement: "I never knew what I was missing by not nursing my first baby. I loved him and I enjoyed him, yes, but I never got so many of the little 'extras' that I get from this one—that little hand that touches my skin as she's nursing, the way she'll pull away from the breast, smile at me and go right back again, the happiness that I feel at being able to give her what she wants."

The "nursing couple"—mother and baby—forge an especially close and interdependent relationship. The baby depends upon his mother for his sustenance and comfort, and the mother looks forward to feeding times to gain a pleasurable sense of closeness with her infant. If a feeding time is too long delayed, both members become distressed: the baby because he is hungry and the mother because her breasts fill with milk. Each member needs the other, yearns for the other, is intimate with the other in a very special way. Because of this unique relationship, many women consider the nursing months among the most fulfilling times of their lives.

WHY SOME WOMEN DECIDE AGAINST BREASTFEEDING

The reasons why women decide not to breastfeed are almost as varied as the arguments in its favor. There are a very, very few instances when a woman cannot nurse her baby—when the mother has a serious infectious illness such as tuberculosis or whooping cough, for example, or when the infant has some condition making it impossible for him to nurse, such as cleft palate. Such cases are rare. Virtually every healthy woman can breastfeed her baby, and as late as 1900, almost every mother did.

Yet, breastfeeding in America has had such a drastic fall from favor that now only one mother in four breastfeeds her baby for the first few days, and less than one out of ten is still nursing him by the time he has attained the ripe age of four months. Surely in our scientifically advanced country, the reasons for this cannot be medical ones. Why, then, do so many mothers decide to substitute the milk of another species for the first-rate infant food already supplied to them?

Like most questions about a major cultural change, this one has no single simple answer. Women say they don't breastfeed because they're too embarrassed, or because the idea doesn't appeal to them, or because they don't want to be tied down, or because there's no reason to, now that ready-made formula is available, or because they're too nervous, or because the whole business just seems too complicated. The real reasons for the swing away from universal breastfeeding to almost universal bottle-feeding in the United States go far deeper than these statements and involve a wide variety of factors. These include the technological advances that spurred reliable refrigeration and a chemical approximation of mother's milk; changes in child-rearing styles; alterations in women's views of their own role; and the emergence of the female breast as a sexual object, with no apparent function other than the delectation of the male.

At the beginning of the twentieth century, psychologists and pediatricians, both members of new and rapidly growing professions, were convinced that babies developed best if they were raised according to certain hard-and-fast rules. Mothers were ordered by their doctors not to feed—or even pick up—their babies oftener than every four hours, no matter how piercing or pathetic the infants' wails. Bottle-feeding was far better adapted to these practices. For breastfeeding requires flexibility, not rigidity; understanding of a baby's needs, not the ability to tell time; and an intuitive maternal reaction, not an adherence to a cultural fad. Also, because the child-care experts insisted that only they knew what was best for the child, mothers believed them—and lost any confidence they might have had in their own maternal capabilities. Lack of confidence itself may be enough to sabotage successful breastfeeding.

At the same time these mothers were being intimidated in the nursery, they were asserting themselves on the street. Demonstrating to achieve the right to vote, smoking cigarettes in public, bobbing their hair, and daring to carve out their own careers, women were eager to free themselves from their traditional roles in the house. And the baby bottle became an instant symbol of emancipation. (Conversely, today's liberationist is just as likely to nurse her baby before going out to picket.)

Later on in the century, the breast was suddenly "discovered" as the most sexual element of a woman's body.

After having been hidden under the tight binders of the flapper era, women's breasts were now molded into fashionable shapes by that new invention, the brassiere. By the time the 1940s came along, pin-up photos were gracing barracks walls, exhibiting the new ideal of feminine beauty—a pretty young woman with enormous breasts. Even the ideal shape of the pectoral area had changed; it now consisted of two pointed cones attached at right angles to the female chest. These unnatural-looking appendages became purely decorative in nature, valued for their sexiness and forgotten for their original function. Husbands began to look upon their wives' breasts as their own property—and some who were married to that rapidly dwindling species of mothers who nursed their babies, became unreasoningly jealous as they saw their little sons or daughters nursing.

Furthermore, as formulas became more satisfactory during the 1930s, the act of giving a bottle achieved a certain status of its own. Mothers who wanted to be modern wanted to bottle-feed. This urge to keep up, to be "modern," is still wooing rural and urban poverty groups away from the breast and to the bottle—with disastrous effects in some underdeveloped countries. When money is scarce, mothers dilute the milk and starve their babies, and when refrigeration and sanitation are inadequate, the milk becomes contaminated. The World Health Organization has mounted a major campaign to encourage women in underdeveloped countries to go back to safe, healthy breastfeeding.

A recent study in Sweden showed that mothers living in modern apartments breastfeed longer than do those living in old-fashioned houses. Nursing, among the best-educated Swedish women, is the "latest thing." In this country, too, change is in the winds. The very women who initially took up the bottle with such enthusiasm—the well-educated, progressive daughters of the middle and upper classes—are now showing greater interest in living their lives the natural way. Today's forward-thinking young woman is less likely to be wearing heavy makeup, an elaborate hairdo, or a padded bra. She is what she is—and is not embarrassed to be herself. She wants to look natural and she wants to act natural. And she is more likely to want to feed her baby according to nature's plan. Yet the modern woman may still have many questions about nursing. The most common questions, with answers based on the most up-to-date medical knowledge, are presented in the next chapter.

You may have all your questions answered, be assured that you can breastfeed your children, yet still be loath to do so. It may still seem like a foreign notion or a repulsive one. It may make you "feel like a cow." If you really do not want to nurse your baby, if the very idea repels you, don't do it. You should not embark upon the nursing adventure because you feel you ought to, to be a good mother. You should not do something you find abhorrent to please your husband, your doctor, your mother, or your best friend. If you do, you are doomed to failure.

How you feel about your baby is vastly more important than how you feed him. A baby raised in a loving home can grow up to be a healthy, psychologically secure individual no matter how he receives his nourishment. While successful nursing is a beautiful, happy experience for both mother and child, the woman who nurses grudgingly because she feels she *should* will probably do more harm to her baby by communicating her feelings of resentment and unhappiness, than she would if she were a relaxed, loving, bottle-feeding mother.

WHAT WILL YOU DO?

What will you do, then? We urge you to give nursing a try. You might look on it as a thirty-day guarantee or your money back. Suppose you begin to nurse your baby and you decide that it's not for you. You haven't lost anything, you haven't invested in anything; you can always stop. The stores will always have those bottles, nipples, sterilizers, and cans of formula. You haven't made a lifelong commitment. You can change your mind.

On the other hand, if you decide to bottle-feed right away, it's much harder to change your mind later. It has been done, by mothers who found that their babies needed breast milk to survive and by women who discovered that bottle-feeding has its own set of problems, but deciding to nurse even after a week has gone by is far from easy. It requires a great deal of determination, persistence, and patience.

Suppose you never gave breastfeeding a chance—don't you think you might look back on this time in later years and wonder whether you and your baby missed one of life's greatest gifts—the bond shared by the nursing couple? The regrets we have in life are less often for the things we have done than for those missed opportunities that will never come again. This priceless chance to nurse your baby comes only once in each baby's lifetime. Make the most of it. You may count these nursing days among the most beautiful and fulfilling of your entire life.

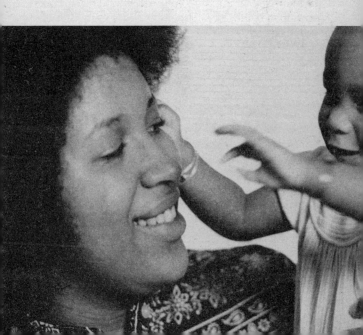

CHAPTER 2.

QUESTIONS THAT MAY BE ON YOUR MIND

Q. Doesn't nursing ruin a woman's figure?

A. No, it does not, even though the fear of getting fat and/ or developing sagging breasts probably deters more women from nursing than any other reason. Many women have breastfed several children and ended up just as slim as they were before they became pregnant. Proper diet during pregnancy and lactation, combined with moderate exercise, will keep you slender.

Any changes that take place in the breasts themselves are due to pregnancy, heredity, and maturity — not lactation. Most women who have borne children do notice that their breasts become somewhat less firm and less erect after childbirth. These changes take place as a result of pregnancy. The extent of the change in breast configuration is determined partly by your heredity, partly by your age, and partly by the amount of weight you gain. One woman may notice little or no change in her breasts, even after giving birth to several children; another may notice a definite droop after bearing only one child.

Generally, the more weight you gain, the more pendulous your breasts will become after you lose these added pounds. However, if you have wisely chosen your ancestors, you may retain your youthful erectness despite childbirth and weight gain.

In any case, the die is cast by the time your first child is born; whether you nurse this child or not will have no effect on your permanent breast conformations. (The temporary effects are highly welcomed by small-breasted women, who find that their increased bust measurements during nursing give them the best figures of their entire lives.)

Dr. Benjamin Segal, a New York obstetrician, likes to point up the truth of these conclusions by referring to a former patient of his. Mae was a Ziegfeld Follies girl, with a beautiful face that matched her exquisite figure. Automatically assuming that Mae would not be interested in breastfeeding, Dr. Segal never discussed the subject with her as he does with most of his patients. Yet the day after Mae's baby was born, he walked into her room and saw her nursing her baby. Mae nursed two subsequent children as well, and ended up with the same lovely figure and beautiful breasts she had had when she was charming New York audiences.

Q. Doesn't a breastfeeding mother have to stay with her baby twenty-four hours a day? I can't bear the thought of being so tied down.

A. Nursing a baby does restrict your freedom somewhat— just as motherhood itself restricts your freedom. You can, however, work out a schedule providing yourself with a great deal of liberty, once your milk supply is established and your baby has developed more regular feeding times. Even working mothers can fit breastfeeding into their schedules.

The overwhelming majority of nursing mothers leave a bottle for the baby before leaving for an occasional afternoon or evening out. The bottle can contain a prepared formula recommended by your pediatrician or your own hand-expressed breast milk. (Advice on leaving these supplementary feedings is given in Chapter Six.)

The first couple of months after childbirth tend to be very confining for breastfeeder and bottle-feeder alike. You will find that you need more rest than you did before you were pregnant, and also that you want to stay near your baby most of the time. Both these needs will keep you close to home. So, even if you plan to go back to work or to resume an active schedule that would make breastfeeding difficult, you can still nurse your baby in his early months.

A few women successfully combine breast- and bottle-feeding on a regular basis. Many a working woman, for example, has her baby-sitter give the infant a bottle every day while Mamma is on the job. Or a father may want to feed the baby in the middle of the night or the early morning, while the mother catches up on her sleep.

Some of these women start to give their babies one bottle a day from the time the babies are a week old. In most cases, however, we would suggest to the woman who wants to regularly combine the two forms of feeding that she wait till her milk supply is well established—say, when the baby is six or eight weeks old. Then, there is less of a chance that the daily bottle will interfere with successful nursing.

The course of breastfeeding almost always runs smoother when the mother provides almost all of the baby's nourishment herself and relies on only an occasional bottle. But combining the two forms of feeding works well for some women, preventing that tied-down feeling.

Q. I like the idea of nursing, but won't it be embarrassing to have to expose my breasts to feed the baby?

A. One of the strongest barriers to more prevalent nursing in our society is the average woman's strong sense of modesty. Taught from early childhood that a proper young lady does not bare her breasts, many a girl grows up with such an exaggerated sense of decorum that she is embarrassed to handle or expose her breasts, even for the specific function they were designed to perform. If you have these feelings, you may worry about feeling embarrassed even when you are alone with your infant. And what will you do, you wonder, when other people are around?

It is a shame that the nursing mother, one of the

loveliest subjects in art or nature, should be such a rarity in modern society. If you had been more accustomed to seeing mothers nurse their babies, you probably would not be so shy about doing it yourself. You can get over these feelings of embarrassment, however. As you start to nurse your baby, insist on strict privacy. Ask the nurse to draw a screen around your hospital bed, and then when you get home, find a quiet nook where no one is likely to disturb you. The chances are, after you have nursed your baby a few times, you will be so gratified by his unselfconscious response that you will find your former embarrassment vanishing.

You may even find yourself among those clever breastfeeding mothers who learn how to purchase, adapt, and manipulate their clothing so that they can maintain their privacy while nursing in such public places as airplanes, department stores, or park benches. Advice on nursing modestly in front of friends or delivery people who suddenly appear at the door is given in Chapter Six.

Q. I hear so many stories about women who really wanted to nurse their babies but had to switch to the bottle because for some reason they couldn't nurse. How can I be sure this won't happen to me?

A. It is true that in our country many women fail at breastfeeding. Many others, however, succeed beautifully. And studies have shown that when encouragement is available from a doctor or hospital that truly believes in the value of breastfeeding, more than 95% of women can successfully nurse their babies. When such medical assistance is lacking, the same kind of reassurance and support can come from a helpful mother or friend—or from an organization like La Leche League.

Q. Doesn't breastfeeding hurt?

A. Some women experience no discomfort at all, but

others do feel some tenderness, usually at the very beginning of nursing as the baby starts to exert pressure on the breasts. This initial soreness, which is most apt to be felt by fair-skinned blondes and redheads, usually goes away in a day or two.

Sore nipples can usually be avoided by toughening them during pregnancy, as suggested in Chapter Four. If the nipples do become tender, however, there are a number of simple measures that will quickly alleviate the discomfort. These measures are described in Chapter Nine.

Q. What happens when the baby's teeth come in?
A. The baby who is nursing properly cannot bite the breast. Some teething babies may try to bite down toward the end of a feeding, after their initial hunger has been satisfied. As little as they are, these infants can and should learn not to do this. Should your baby try it, say NO in a sharp voice and take him off the breast immediately. After getting this reaction a couple of times, he will learn not to bite.

Sioux Indian mothers still thump their babies on the head when they bite the breast. The babies turn blue in the face with rage—but they learn not to bite. You can no doubt accomplish the same result by gentler means.

Q. Why do some women have milk and not others?
A. Anthropologists and doctors alike testify that every woman who has ever had a baby has had milk come into her breasts. The functioning of the let-down reflex, as explained in Chapter Three, may be somewhat inhibited in certain women in certain circumstances, but every woman gets milk and virtually every woman can get this milk to her baby.

Q. My mother didn't have enough milk to nurse me. Will I take after her?
A. The ability to be a good breastfeeder is not something

you inherit. Virtually all cases of insufficient milk supply are due to mismanagement of one sort or another and to lack of encouragement from doctors, hospitals, family, and friends. Your mother may not have had enough milk because at the time you were born, breast-feeding was "out of style" with many doctors and nurses. Today there is a renewed realization that breastfeeding is still superior to all its imitations, and we have relearned the old ways of building up your milk supply, which you can learn about in Chapter Six.

Q. I'm almost perfectly flat-chested. How could my breasts possibly hold enough milk to nourish a baby?

A. The size of the breasts has no relation at all to their efficiency as milk producers. Size is determined by the amount of fatty tissue in the mammary glands. Since this fatty tissue is not at all involved in the process of making or ejecting milk, small breasts are not an obstacle to feeding a baby. Many small-bosomed women nurse their babies successfully, and some even donate extra milk to milk banks for the benefit of sick or premature babies. See Chapter Three for a detailed explanation of how the breasts make and give milk.

Q. How can I tell if my milk is rich enough for the baby?

A. Your milk will have enough of all essential elements your baby needs. Don't worry about its bluish, watery appearance—that's what human milk is supposed to look like. Milk is almost the same from one woman to another, and the differences that do exist are unimportant. The chances are, even if you were undernourished or sick, your milk would still contain all the nutrients your baby needs for his first few months of life.

Q. Suppose my milk doesn't agree with the baby?

A. Breast milk agrees with every baby. No baby is allergic to it. No baby rejects it in favor of a formula. On the contrary, there are infants—premature babies with immature digestive systems or others with specific digestive disturbances—who thrive *only* on breast milk.

Q. I've always been "the nervous type" and I hear you have to be calm to breastfeed. Am I doomed to failure?

A. It is true that a calm, relaxed mother usually has an easier time at breastfeeding than does a tense, nervous one. And during times of emotional upset, the flow of milk may be considerably decreased due to an inhibition of the let-down reflex. The quality of the milk, though, is unchanged.

The very act of holding her baby and putting him to the breast has a relaxing effect on many a woman. This is probably due to the action of the hormones released by the process of lactation. In fact, Dr. Evelyn B. Thoman of the Stanford University School of Medicine has found that female rats fight less and maintain their body temperature better when they are lactating, and that, in general, they respond less to stressful situations at this time.

This moderation of the nursing mother's responses is probably nature's way of protecting babies from any extreme changes in maternal behavior caused by outside stresses. So, you may be among the many "nervous types" who find a new calmness as they embark upon the nursing adventure.

If you find it hard to relax when you start to nurse, you can be helped. The administration of a nasal hormone spray triggers the let-down reflex for some women, helping their milk to flow. And in Chapter Six, you will find a few tricks that can help you relax before a feeding.

Knowing that your baby is getting a good supply of milk can be the most reassuring tranquilizer of all. (Some dairy farmers feel that their high-strung cows, once they start to give milk, are the most productive in the barn.)

Q. I want to breastfeed, but my husband isn't overjoyed about the idea. Is it worth making an issue about this?

A. Only you can decide how strongly your husband feels about your breastfeeding, how much of his opinion is based on lack of knowledge (which you can help to correct), and whether nursing your baby means enough to you to take a stand.

The reassurance of a supportive husband is often vital to a successful breastfeeding experience, and so you may want to defer to your husband's wishes. On the other hand, you might point out to your husband the advantages of nursing—including the bonus feature that he won't be called upon to get up in the middle of the night to feed the baby. You might also suggest that he read Chapters Seven and Eight of this book.

Many a husband initially opposed to his wife's breastfeeding has found a new pride in her femininity as he watched her nurse his baby.

Q. Ever since I decided to breastfeed, everyone has been trying to talk me out of it. How can I deal with all this opposition?

A. Opposition to breastfeeding is very common. Sometimes it is quite outspoken, as expressed by the mother who

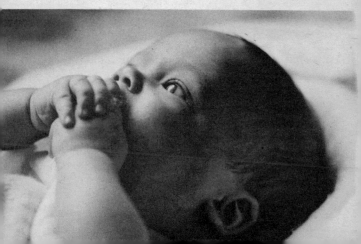

disgustedly asked her daughter, "Why can't you be like everybody else and do the *natural* thing—give the baby a bottle?" Or it can be more subtly expressed by neighbors who say, "What? Are you *still* nursing?" Or by baby nurses who blame every little upset on mother's milk—either it's too rich or not rich enough, or you're starving him or overfeeding him. Or by the doctor who suggests that you stop breastfeeding whenever you run into a minor problem.

When these situations arise, try to think why these people react the way they do. Often someone who offers objections has good intentions but poor information about the normal course of breastfeeding. If so, you can enlighten him or her. Sometimes a trace of jealousy affects the grandmother who sees you care for your baby so competently without her, or the neighbor who was an unsuccessful nursing mother herself. If this seems to be the case, try to say something to build up the individual's morale. And sometimes a busy doctor who has seen many women start to nurse and then give it up, may really be convinced that the modern woman has lost her ability to breastfeed. You can demonstrate to him that this isn't so.

In any case, once you make your decision to breastfeed, stick to it. You may not be able to change the minds of others, but you don't have to let them change your mind, either.

Q. How will my older children react to my breastfeeding the baby?

A. They will respond to your own attitude. If you let them know that you are doing the right thing by breastfeeding, they will accept this as the way things are. If, on the other hand, you feel guilty and afraid of making them jealous, they will sense your vulnerability and will capitalize on it. For more about emphasizing the positive with the older brothers and sisters of a nursing baby, see Chapter Six.

Q. I hate milk. Do I have to drink a quart a day to make milk?

A. You don't have to drink a quart a day—or a pint—or even a cup, if you don't want to. While milk is an excellent source of protein, minerals, and vitamins, many other foods can be substituted for it. See Chapter Four.

Q. Do I have to eat special foods while I'm nursing?

A. That depends on what kind of diet you have been following. If you have been eating a variety of healthful foods, rich in proteins and vitamins, you need not change your eating habits—except to eat enough extra to make up for the 1,000 or so calories leaving your body in the milk. If your diet has been deficient, however, this is a good time to make a change. Suggestions for a well-balanced diet during pregnancy and lactation are given in Chapter Four.

Occasionally you will find that certain foods you eat in quantity—particularly such gas-producing foods as cabbage or brussels sprouts—may give both you and your baby gas. Or you may feel that your baby is especially wakeful after you have been drinking a lot of coffee. If something like this happens, you can cut back on the foods in question while you are nursing. Some babies don't react to any foods, however, so it's mostly a matter of trying everything and seeing what happens.

Be sensible, though. One mother called her pediatrician and said that her baby was fussy. She wondered whether it could be due to the fact that she had eaten chocolate the night before. The doctor asked her what she had eaten and she told him, "Half a cake." It is surprising she wasn't on the phone to her own doctor!

Q. How can I nurse if I have inverted nipples?

A. Many nipples that appear inverted or pushed in, work themselves out during pregnancy so that they are able to function normally after the baby is born. Sometimes exercises during pregnancy, involving "nipple rolling" will help to bring out such nipples. Other cases are helped by the wearing of special breast shields. These measures are all described in Chapter Four. True inverted nipples that will not respond to any of these measures are extremely rare. Even in such cases, a baby can occasionally grab hold of the areola and manage to get the milk, despite the lack of a protractile nipple.

Q. Suppose my baby is born by Caesarean section? Can I still nurse?

A. Yes, the milk comes in just as quickly after a Caesarean operation as it does after a normal delivery. You may not feel up to nursing as soon as you would otherwise, but after a day or so, you can start to nurse successfully. You will probably want to rest more at home, and this will have only good effects on your milk supply. More about this in Chapter Nine.

Q. Can I nurse my baby when I am menstruating? I've heard that milk given at this time isn't good for the baby.

A. You may not menstruate at all while you are nursing. If you do menstruate, however, there is no reason not to nurse your baby while you are having your period. You may find that the hormonal changes connected with the menstrual cycle may temporarily diminish your supply of milk. If this happens, just nurse more frequently. In any case, only the quantity will be affected—not the quality.

Q. Does nursing a baby really prevent pregnancy?

A. The definitive answer to this question is—"sometimes." Based on records in primitive societies where long-term lactation is the rule, and on studies of nursing, partially-nursing, and non-nursing mothers in this country, we can point to some evidence that breast-feeding postpones pregnancy. There are so many qualifications and exceptions, however, that you should put your trust in some other method of contraception if you want to space your babies. You should not take oral contraceptives, however, for reasons explained in Chapter Four.

Generally, if your baby is living solely on breast milk—receiving no supplemental bottles nor any solid food—the hormonal balance in your body will prevent ovulation and therefore pregnancy. Generally, you will have one "sterile" menstrual period before you begin to ovulate. But don't depend on it. Women have become pregnant while fully lactating and before they have resumed menstruation. So be prepared—and you won't be surprised.

Q. If I do become pregnant, can I still nurse my baby?

A. You can continue to breastfeed, although it is probable that your milk supply will diminish somewhat after the first few months of your pregnancy. While an occasional woman will nurse one child right through pregnancy and up to the birth of a second child, and then come home to nurse both, this is usually not a good idea. Lactation and pregnancy both demand a certain amount of strength from the mother; the two of them together may take too much of a toll.

Q. Suppose I have a premature baby who has to stay in the hospital for several weeks? How could I possibly nurse him?

A. Many mothers give their milk to their premature babies by hand-expressing or pumping the milk from the breasts and taking it to the hospital every day until the infants can nurse at their mothers' bosoms. These tiny babies usually thrive best on breast milk, and so their mothers feel it is well worth the extra effort to maintain their supply of milk until the baby comes home to nurse normally. More about expressing and pumping in Chapter Nine.

Q. What is La Leche League?
A. This is a remarkable organization set up for the sole purpose of helping nursing mothers. La Leche ("the milk" in Spanish) was founded in 1956, when seven mothers got together to see how women who were successfully breastfeeding could best help other mothers with questions or problems. Fifteen years later, the League comprises more than 1000 groups around the world, with nearly fifty doctors on its medical advisory board.

The League publishes a bi-monthly newsletter, and it holds biennial international conventions and monthly small-group meetings. It is available twenty-four hours a day to anxious mothers facing life-or-death crises or minor problems, and is a constant source of help to any nursing mother.

To become a League member and to find out the address of the group closest to you, write to La Leche League International, 9616 Minneapolis Avenue, Franklin Park, Illinois 60131. If you live in a major metropolitan area, look for the League in your local telephone directory.

Q. Is the DDT content in breast milk harmful to babies?
A. Many women have been alarmed by such "scare" reports as a poster showing a sign on the breast of a pregnant woman that reads "Caution: Keep Out of the Reach of Children" and adds, "Milk in Such Containers May be Unfit for Human Consumption," or the ad for an "ecological" newsletter that states, "Doctors now suggest infants should not drink their mothers' milk."

Such misleading statements completely distort the truth—which is that *there is absolutely no medical evidence that breastfed babies suffer any ill effects from the DDT levels in their mothers' milk.*

The facts in the DDT situation are these:

- Human milk does contain DDT, as does the milk of every mammalian species that has been investigated.
- The DDT concentration in milk fat bears a constant ratio to that in body fat, which in turn reflects the average DDT intake in the individual's diet.
- By strictly controlling cattle feed, we can reduce the level of DDT in cow's milk to less than one part per million. Since human beings have a much more diversified and harder-to-control diet than do cows, the DDT levels in human fat and in human milk are higher.
- Even if a mother gave her baby cow's milk instead of breast milk, the concentration of DDT in the baby's body fat would still not drop to the level in cattle for two reasons. First of all, the fetus acquires a higher level even before birth, as a reflection of his mother's diet. And secondly, when foods other than milk assume a prominent place in the child's diet, his DDT level will reach the adult level.
- While some human milk has been shown to contain DDT at levels higher than that allowed in milk for commercial sale, this commercially acceptable rate is an extremely conservative one. It represents only about *one ten-thousandth* of the dose needed to produce acute DDT poisoning.
- Scientists who have studied DDT levels in milk have stated repeatedly that the advantages of breastfeeding far outweigh the presence of DDT in breast milk and that no baby should be taken off the breast because of the DDT factor.
- In a personal letter to La Leche League, Dr. Göran Löfroth, the Swedish toxicologist who originally made the widely quoted statements about DDT in breast milk, wrote: "I personally believe that human milk, when available, is superior to formula milk— and consequently the solution of the problem is not

to abandon breast-feeding and human milk, but instead to decrease and eventually stop the use of DDT and similar persistent chemicals."

- Nobody is saying that DDT is good for you and your baby. To minimize the amount of DDT in your body and in your milk, avoid pesticides as much as possible, especially the aerosol sprays containing DDT or other "hard" pesticides. Get rid of bugs by swatting when possible. If you must use pesticides, use those in non-spray form that do not contain DDT or its close relatives, DDD or DDE. Stay away from places where these pesticides are used.

CHAPTER 3.

THE MIRACLE OF LACTATION

This chapter deals with some of the medical and scientific aspects of breastfeeding: how the breasts make the milk and get it to the baby, how lactation may postpone menstruation and pregnancy, and what the chemical compositions are for colostrum, breast milk, and cow's milk. Because of the subject matter, some of this material is rather technical. You may want to skim through it and read only those parts that answer your questions, or look back later as questions arise. If you do read it all, we feel you will agree that lactation, the process by which a mother feeds her newborn baby with the milk produced by her own body, is truly a miracle of biological design.

THE DEVELOPMENT OF THE BREASTS

To understand how the breasts develop and function, we have to know a little bit about our bodies' glandular systems. Those parts of the human body that develop secretions are called glands. The endocrine glands (*endo* means within) secrete powerful chemical substances called hormones that go directly into the bloodstream and travel through it to affect other parts of the body. These hormones influence such basic processes as growth, sexual development, and even the formation of personality. The exocrine glands (*exo* means outside) secrete substances into ducts that carry them elsewhere in the body. The breasts are exocrine glands that are stimulated, both in their development and in their production of milk, by the hormones of the endocrine glands.

These mammary glands, as the breasts are medically termed, got their name from *mamma,* the Latin word for breast. Most likely, the Romans got their word from their babies who closely associated their mothers with their source of food and directed their first word to both.

Your mammary glands began to develop when you were a six-week-old embryo in your own mother's womb; the main milk ducts in your breasts were already formed by the time you were born. Right after birth, your breasts may even have been swollen and excreting a small amount of milk, known as "witch's milk." This very common phenomenon among both boy and girl infants which subsides after a few days, is caused by the stimulation of the infant's mammary glands by the same hormones produced by the placenta to prepare the mother's breasts for lactation. From then, your mammary glands were inactive until shortly before the onset of puberty, when hormones began to flood your body.

CHANGES OF PUBERTY

Your body then took its first step toward changing from that of a girl to a woman when your pituitary gland, the "master gland" of the endocrine system, sent a message to your female sex glands, the ovaries, directing them to make *estrogen* in sharply increased amounts. Estrogen is the principal female hormone, the substance responsible for the growth of female-patterned body hair, for the sexual maturation of the genital organs, and for the development of feminine contours, including the swelling of the breasts. The pituitary gland also stimulated the manufacture of other female hormones, most notably *progesterone,* a hormone that actively prepares the body for pregnancy.

A combination of growth hormones and female sex hormones spurred the development of your breasts throughout your adolescence, until you reached your full body growth sometime in your late teens or early twenties.

THE ANATOMY OF THE BREASTS

Your breasts are delicate organs made up of a combination

of glandular tissue, supporting connective tissue, and protective fatty tissue. Just as women differ in height, in general body build and in facial characteristics, they vary considerably in regard to the size and shape of their breasts. These characteristics are not important as far as feeding a baby is concerned. Whether your breasts are broad or narrow, rounded or conical, high or sloping, you can still nurse your baby. The size of your breasts is just as irrelevant to the feeding function as their shape. Size is determined by the amount of fatty tissue in the breasts, and since the only purpose of this tissue is to encase and protect the more functional elements, it has no bearing at all on your ability to produce milk. You can be an excellent nurser, no matter what the size or shape of your breasts.

THE NIPPLE

Let us look at the breasts with a baby's-eye view. The nipple is the handle by which the infant grabs hold of the breast, and also the spout through which he receives his milk. Each nipple, which may be cylindrical in some women and conical in others, has fifteen to twenty tiny openings through which the milk is excreted. The nipple is well supplied with nerve endings. Their stimulation by the nursing baby induces the uterine contractions which help return that organ to its pre-pregnancy size. The nipple is also amply supplied with blood vessels, which cause it to become firm and erect when stimulated by cold, by sexual excitation, or by tactile stimulation such as the mouth movements of the nursing baby.

THE AREOLA

Surrounding the nipple is a circle called the areola. During pregnancy, glands in the areola known as Montgomery's glands become enlarged and look like little pimples. They remain quite noticeable throughout pregnancy and lactation, when they secrete a substance that lubricates and protects the nipple during nursing. After lactation, these glands recede to their former unobtrusive state.

The areola and nipple are darker than the rest of the breast, ranging from a light pink in very fair-skinned women to a very dark brown in others. The areolar pigmentation deepens in pregnancy and remains darker during lactation, after which the color fades somewhat; it never reverts, however, to the lighter shade it was before pregnancy. (This is one way doctors sometimes determine whether a woman has ever borne a child.) The darker color of the areola may be some sort of visual signal to the newborn infant, since he must close his mouth upon the areola, not upon the nipple alone, if he is to obtain any milk.

THE MILK-MAKING APPARATUS

Directly beneath and behind the areola is a group of milk pools, upon which the suckling baby puts pressure. These pools, known scientifically as lactiferous sinuses, are widened parts of the lactiferous ducts, or milk-carrying canals, which transport the milk to the nipples.

The Breast

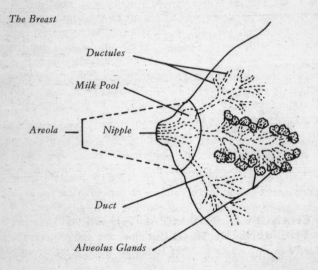

Ductules

Milk Pool

Areola — Nipple

Duct

Alveolus Glands

There are from fifteen to twenty ducts, each of which empties into the nipple. At their other ends within the breast, the ducts branch off into smaller canals called ductules. At the end of each ductule is a grape-like cluster of tiny rounded sacs called alveoli, in which the milk is made. Both the ducts and the alveoli are lined with cells that contract to squeeze the milk into and through the duct system. Each cluster of alveoli is referred to as a lobule (a word that means a small rounded organ), and a cluster of lobules is called a lobe. The lobes, each of which is a gland in miniature, are at the base of the breast next to the chest. There are from fifteen to twenty lobes in each breast, each lobe connected to one duct, each duct emptying into one nipple opening.

THE SUPPORTING STRUCTURE

The breast is supported by the muscles attached to the ribs, the collarbone, and the bones of the upper arm near the shoulder. External support can also come from a well-fitting bra. While wearing a bra or going without one has no effect at all upon the breastfeeding function, the force of gravity will tend to pull down the heavier breasts of the pregnant or nursing woman. A good bra will help to prevent undue stretching of the suspensory ligaments of the upper part of the breast. Breasts that are wide at the base tend to remain more erect, and some doctors feel that a broad-breasted woman will retain her figure, whether or not she wears a bra.

In some cultures, women deliberately pull at their breasts to make them longer, so that it will be easier to nurse a baby strapped to the mother's back. Since this is not your aim, you would probably have the best chance for preserving your figure if you wear a good bra, even for sleep, during the latter part of your pregnancy and during lactation.

CHANGES IN THE BREASTS DURING THE MENSTRUAL CYCLE

From the time you reach the menarche (your first menstrual period) until you arrive at the menopause, a rhythmic cycle regulates your body. Every month your system produces a series of hormones that prepares your body to bear children. Among these preparations are the thickening of the uterine lining and an increase in the blood supply. In the months you do not conceive, these preparations are washed away at the time of the menses. Ever optimistic, however, your body begins the entire cycle anew the next month.

The female sex hormones, estrogen and progesterone, produce changes in your breasts in hopes that this will be the month that sperm and egg will find each other to create a new being. Just before you menstruate, your breasts may enlarge and may also feel tender. This is because the high levels of estrogen in your body make the blood vessels and gland ducts in the breasts grow somewhat during this premenstrual phase, in preparation for a possible pregnancy. (While the estrogen stimulates growth, it inhibits the production of milk. This is why your breasts will not begin to produce milk until after the birth of your baby and the delivery of the placenta.) Once menstruation begins, the breasts quickly return to their previous state. If, however, you become pregnant, the heightened levels of sex hormones in your body produce many changes in your breasts.

CHANGES IN THE BREASTS DURING PREGNANCY

When you first go to the doctor to have your pregnancy confirmed, he will perform a pelvic examination and will also closely examine your breasts to look for signs that you have indeed conceived. Some of these signs that appear by the fifth or sixth week of pregnancy include a persistent fullness and tenderness of the breasts similar to the premenstrual sensations, the sudden prominence of the glands of Montgomery, and the enlargement and darkening of both the nipples and areolae.

While the main milk ducts have been in the breast since

you were first born, the complete duct system develops only now, when you are pregnant. It is completed during the first six months of pregnancy, and by the time your baby is born, glandular tissue has almost completely replaced the fatty tissue in your breasts. The development of this glandular tissue is responsible for the enlargement of the breasts during pregnancy and lactation. By the time your baby is born, each of your breasts will have gained about a pound and a half of additional weight.

The placenta, that organ that transmits nourishment and oxygen from your system to your unborn baby's, also has another function. It is a chemical factory that in early pregnancy takes over from your ovaries the job of producing large amounts of hormones. Somewhere around the fifth month of your pregnancy, the placenta begins to produce a new hormone called *human placental lactogen,* which stimulates the development of the alveoli, the milk sacs. Once these are formed, your breasts begin to produce "early milk," or colostrum, a colorless or slightly yellowish liquid that may occasionally drip from your nipples during the latter part of your pregnancy.

CHANGES IN THE BREASTS AFTER CHILDBIRTH

Once your baby has been born and the placenta has been delivered, the estrogen and progesterone levels in your body drop sharply. After delivery another hormone, *prolactin,* is released into your system. Your pituitary gland has been producing prolactin all your life, but its release has been blocked by an inhibitory factor in your brain. The only time this factor does not inhibit the release of prolactin is immediately after you give birth and for as long as an infant is suckling at your breasts. Prolactin causes the mammary glands to produce milk. It also seems to have psychological effects, since laboratory experiments have found that it can induce motherly behavior, even when artificially administered to virgin animals.

The changed hormonal balance in your body sets in motion a chain of events necessary for successful lactation. Extra blood is pumped into the small blood vessels of the alveoli, causing these vessels to enlarge and become visible beneath the skin, and making the breasts firmer and fuller. The manufacture of milk and the vascular expansion are responsible for the engorgement and temporary discomfort experienced by some—but not all—women. It is almost always relieved by the baby's early and frequent nursing.

(The woman who does not nurse her baby is likely to experience a great deal of discomfort from this engorgement, which in her case may last from twenty-four to thirty-six hours. She may develop throbbing pains in the breasts and under the arms, as well as fever and headache. She is generally advised to wear a firm brassiere and to take a mild pain reliever like aspirin. The doctor may prescribe estrogenic hormone preparations either by mouth or by injection to inhibit lactation. The strongest factor in drying up her milk, however, will be the lack of stimulation to the breasts. If a baby does not nurse and the milk is not otherwise expressed, the alveoli will get the message that they are not needed. Within a few days, they will stop producing milk.)

Immediately after birth, the cells in the center of the alveoli undergo fatty degeneration, and are eliminated in the first milk as colostrum. At any point from as soon as twelve hours after birth to as late as four days afterwards, the colostrum is replaced by the true milk. Generally, the sooner and more frequently the baby is put to the breast, the sooner the milk will come in. The milk will also come in sooner for the woman who has previously nursed one or more babies, since the duct system in her breasts is already stretched and better able to transport the milk to the milk pools, where the baby can get at it.

THE LET-DOWN REFLEX—HOW THE BABY GETS THE MILK

The woman whose let-down reflex is operating well is

usually overjoyed, not "let down" in the usual sense. This was originally a dairy term, referring to the cow's ability to "let down" her milk. Also known as the milk-ejection reflex and, in England, the "draught" (pronounced "draft"), the let-down is responsible for getting the milk to the baby.

As the baby suckles, he stimulates the nerve endings in your nipples, which then send signals to the pituitary gland, directing it to continue to produce the hormone prolactin. The prolactin signals the alveoli to produce milk. As long as the breasts are suckled, they will continue to make milk. The baby's suckling also causes the pituitary to release another hormone, *oxytocin*. Oxytocin travels through the bloodstream to the breast, where it causes the little cells lining the alveoli to contract, thereby squeezing the milk from the alveoli into the ducts. As the milk enters the ducts, the cells along the walls of the ducts also contract, sending the milk out to the milk pools beneath the areolae. So while prolactin makes the milk, oxytocin makes it available to the baby. (Oxytocin also causes the uterus to contract during lactation, during orgasm, and during childbirth.)

When you first start to nurse your baby, it will take anywhere from several seconds to several minutes of the baby's suckling to produce the let-down reflex. After it has been established, you may find that hearing your baby cry or even just thinking about him will bring it on. Some of the signs of the let-down reflex are a tingling sensation in the breast, the dripping of milk before the baby starts to nurse, the release of milk from the nipple other than the one the baby is suckling, cramps caused by the contractions of the uterus, and the relief of nipple discomfort as the baby nurses. Once lactation is well established, milk may spray from an uncovered breast for a distance of several feet at the onset of the let-down reflex.

The Renaissance artist Jacopo Tintoretto portrayed a beautiful representation of the let-down reflex in his work, "The Origin of the Milky Way." The painting tells the story of Herakles, Zeus' son by a mortal woman, whom Zeus put to the breast of the sleeping goddess Hera to make immortal. After the infant had stopped drinking of Hera's milk, the milk continued to flow from the goddess's breasts. Some went up into the sky, forming the galaxy, and the rest dropped on the ground, forming a garden of lilies. The British scientist S. J. Folley points out that this picture illustrates two important attributes of the milk-ejection reflex: first, that the stimulus of suckling creates an increased pressure of the milk inside the breasts, causing it to spurt from the nipples, and secondly, that even though only one breast may be suckled, milk will flow from both.

In recent years, hormone preparations available in the form of a nasal spray or a tablet held in the mouth have been administered by some doctors to women whose let-down may be a bit slow in getting started. While this may be a help to some nervous, high-strung women, many doctors feel that it is unnecessary and that any woman, if she gives herself time, will develop an adequate let-down reflex.

The let-down reflex has a strong psychological base. The pituitary gland, which controls the release of oxytocin, is itself controlled by the hypothalamus. This walnut-sized organ in the brain is often referred to as the "seat of emotion," since it receives messages about the individual's psychological state and, acting on these messages, sends its own orders to the glands, translating emotions into physiological reactions. The emotions, therefore, exert a powerful influence on such hormone-regulated functions as the menstrual cycle, childbirth, and lactation.

Most nursing failures you hear about can be attributed to a failure of the let-down reflex to function normally. Pain, embarrassment, or distraction can inhibit this reflex and hold your milk back from your baby. If your nipples hurt you, your let-down won't work right. If you are distressed by the disparaging remarks of relatives and friends, your let-down will let you down. If you overtire yourself, don't eat properly, don't respect your own needs for privacy and for relaxation, you may make the milk—but you may not be able to get it to your baby.

This is why it is so important to prepare yourself for nursing, both physically and emotionally. Chances are that even if you did nothing and knew nothing, you might still be blessed with good milk production and an active milk-ejection reflex. But the more you know about the "womanly art of breastfeeding," and the better you can prepare yourself for this maternal activity, the better will be your chances for success.

MENSTRUATION, OVULATION, AND PREGNANCY

The baby's continued suckling at the breast maintains high levels of prolactin in the mother's system. The prolactin tends to suppress the action of the ovaries, preventing them from producing the hormones that trigger ovulation or the release of eggs. The woman who is not ovulating cannot become pregnant.

Most women do not ovulate (or menstruate) at all while their babies are receiving no food other than breast milk. As soon as supplementary bottles or solid food are added to the diet, though, the baby's sucking becomes less vigorous and the prolactin level in the mother's system drops. If there is not enough prolactin to inhibit ovarian function, the mother again begins her regular ovulatory and menstrual cycles. She may have one "sterile" menstrual period before ovulation begins; that is, she may begin to menstruate but not yet be able to conceive. Or, on the other hand, she may be fertile with her first menses after childbirth.

Some women do not begin to ovulate and menstruate for several months after their babies are completely weaned from the breast. Others, however, may ovulate even while they are fully lactating—and before their menses resume. So, while you are *less likely* to conceive when your baby is totally breastfed, you *might* become pregnant. Since it is impossible to tell when a particular woman will begin to ovulate, the use of mechanical contraceptive devices is recommended for women who want to space their children.

COLOSTRUM, THE EARLY MILK

The first time your baby is put to the breast, he will be drinking colostrum, that clear or yellowish fluid that has been produced by your breasts since the latter part of your pregnancy. While it is similar to true milk, it is somewhat different in composition, containing more protein, minerals, vitamin A and nitrogen, and less fat and sugar than true milk. Since it is easier for the baby to digest and to utilize than milk, colostrum is an ideal first food. One important function is its laxative effect in cleaning out the meconium from your baby's bowels. This is greenish-black waste matter formed in the baby's intestinal tract while he is in your uterus.

Within the past ten years, more than thirty components have been identified in human colostrum, thirteen of which are unique to breast milk, but aside from its known nutritional and cathartic values, we don't really know whether colostrum has any additional benefits. Some animals are known to receive immunity from certain diseases by drinking their mothers' colostrum that contains antibodies against specific bacteria and viruses. Antibodies from colostrum have been found in the feces of human infants who have been breastfed but not in those of infants who have received formula. Some doctor-researchers are convinced that the antibodies found in human colostrum cannot be absorbed through an infant's intestinal tract, and therefore cannot confer any immunological benefits on him. Yet others feel that the breastfed baby's superior resistance to disease is in part due to these very antibodies. Perhaps some day, one or the other of these camps will prove its point beyond question. Meanwhile, we can be assured that colostrum is a good food and that no baby is being shortchanged by being given colostrum until the "real thing" comes along.

THE MILK

Throughout your youngster's childhood, milk will probably

be his single most valuable food, since it contains a large helping of the vitamins, minerals, fats, and carbohydrates essential to his diet. The milk of every mammal has the same basic structure, but there are striking differences among the milks of various species. It seems reasonable to suppose that the milk of each species is especially suited to the needs of its young. The whale, for example, gives milk rich in fats and calories—elements important for survival in cold water. The milk of the rabbit is high in protein, which is important for the rapid growth of young rabbits. Even though we are constantly learning more about the unique structure of human milk, we will probably never be able to identify every single one of its more than 100 different components, which differ in chemical composition and proportion from the components of every other kind of milk. Over the last ten years, more than 300 scientific papers have been published on the biochemical properties of human milk.

While we cannot report here on *all* the unique properties of human milk, we can briefly list some of the differences between cow's milk and mothers' milk.

With its slightly bluish cast, breast milk looks thinner than cow's milk. Well, people are thinner than cows, and this is the way people's milk is supposed to look. Toward the end of a feeding when the fat content of human milk is higher, it does take on a somewhat creamier appearance.

Both milks contain a large share of vitamins, although the amounts vary considerably, with human milk containing many more units of vitamins A and E than cow's milk, and fewer of vitamins D and K. Neither milk contains enough vitamin D for a baby's needs, so he will have to get this vitamin in the form of drops, unless he is out in the sunshine every day, in which case he can synthesize his own vitamin D. Cow's milk contains practically no vitamin C, but a mother who eats a well-balanced diet will produce her baby's minimum daily requirement in her milk.

Human milk contains twice as much iron as raw cow's

milk, but neither one contains enough to satisfy the baby's needs after he has reached the age of five or six months, by which time he has used up the stores of iron he was born with. Cow's milk contains about four times the amount of calcium, six times the phosphorus, and twice as much sulfur as human milk. The bottle-fed baby excretes a large portion of these minerals as excess.

Cow's milk contains more than twice as much protein as human milk, but in a form that the baby utilizes much less efficiently, probably because cow's milk contains very few nucleotides, those factors that make it possible for proteins to be synthesized. Human milk contains a great variety of nucleotides.

Breast milk contains twice the amount of sugar as cow's milk. The type of sugar it contains may be responsible for the acidity of the breastfed baby's intestinal tract and the absence of many bacteria that apparently cannot live in an acid environment.

In recent years, doctors have been investigating the effects of saturated fats upon the body's cholesterol level, in an attempt to find a relationship between diet and heart disease. While a definite relationship between a diet high in saturated fats and a tendency toward heart disease has not been established beyond doubt, there is a strong suspicion that such a relationship may exist. It is worth noting that, while cow's milk and human milk contain similar amounts of fat, breast milk is lower in saturated fats.

Aware of the differences between human milk and raw cow's milk, manufacturers of formula products use the latest scientific knowledge as a guideline for the preparation of nutritionally sound baby formulas. Some companies modify the cow's milk to try to imitate the chemical analysis and physical characteristics of human milk, while others aim to achieve the nutritional results of human milk without copying its exact chemical analysis (an impossibility, in any case).

One formula manufacturer, J. B. Roerig and Co., has expressed its philosophy this way:

The normal breast fed infant receiving adequate quantities of milk from a healthy well nourished mother will automatically be provided with all of his nutritional requirements except Vitamin D. However, the infant who is fed on a cow milk formula is another matter and care must be taken to see that adequate amounts of all the necessary nutrients are provided either in the formula or as a supplement.

To provide these nutrients, formula makers use tables of recommended minimum daily requirements—and all their ingenuity. Most formulas, for example, replace the butterfat in cow's milk with some combination of oleo, soy oil, corn oil, coconut oil, palm oil, olive oil, or peanut oil. They experiment with various types of sugars, add substances to help the baby's body to synthesize some of the unsaturated fatty acids, and in other ways try to copy the values of breast milk. From time to time, however, scientists discover new elements in breast milk, requiring new modifications of cow's milk. As recently as 1966, six new ingredients were discovered, and it is most probable that, with all our scientific knowhow, we will never be able to isolate, identify, and copy all the constitutents of breast milk—the best milk for the human infant.

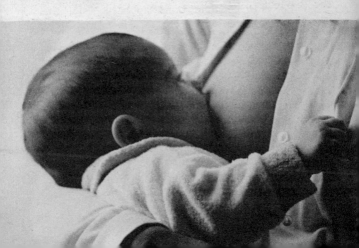

CHAPTER 4.

THE CARE AND FEEDING OF THE MOTHER

Long before you feel your baby's first stirrings inside your womb, you can—and should—prepare to be a successful breastfeeder. Early and thorough prenatal care will contribute to the health of both you and your baby, and will go a long way toward making your postnatal period a happier one. If you care for your breasts with an eye toward breastfeeding, you will be better able to nurse. Finally, if you are well informed about what to expect during labor and delivery, you will be more apt to have a happy childbirth experience, and studies have shown that the easier a woman's delivery, the more enthusiastic she will be about breastfeeding.

You may already have a family doctor who takes care of you and your husband, who will deliver your baby and who will then take care of him, too. If not, you will probably want to look for an obstetrician-gynecologist, a doctor who specializes in treating women and in delivering babies, and later a pediatrician, a doctor who specializes in taking care of children. The most important thing you will look for in either one is medical competence. If a physician has staff privileges with an accredited hospital, you can feel confident that he is an able practitioner. How can you tell whether he is enthusiastic about the benefits of breastfeeding and knowledgeable about its management? There are several ways you might find out.

CHOOSING YOUR OBSTETRICIAN

In seeking an obstetrician, you can choose your hospital first (see next section) and ask the director of obstetrics and gynecology for the name of a doctor who encourages breastfeeding. You might also speak to your family doctor, your friends who have been happy with their childbirth experiences, or a local representative of one of the organizations especially formed to educate women about childbirth and breastfeeding.*

Call the first doctor on your list and ask his secretary whether you can make an appointment for a consultation. If so, find out the fee for that, as compared to a complete examination. Or else just go in for an examination but be sure to spend some time talking to the doctor. Ask him how he feels about breastfeeding and how many of his patients nurse their babies. (The higher the percentage, the more helpful he is likely to be.) Ask about anything else that is on your mind, such as how he feels about unmedicated deliveries, about permitting your husband to remain with you during labor and delivery, and what his fees are. If you feel that you can have confidence in this doctor, your shopping is over. If, however, you are not completely convinced, you don't have to say anything yet. Meet the other physicians on your list and then make up your mind. You can always call the offices of those doctors you decide against, tell the secretary that you will be going to someone else, and ask her to send you a bill for the single examination or consultation.

You may find that you are not 100% happy with any of the physicians you meet; maybe none of the doctors in your area are both enthusiastic and knowledgeable about breastfeeding. Remember that a supportive doctor is helpful, but he is not essential to your success in breastfeeding. If you find an obstetrician whom you like in other respects, you don't have to drop him because of his shortcomings on the topic of

---

* Call or write any of the following for the names of local representatives:

La Leche League International, 9616 Minneapolis Ave., Franklin Park, Illinois 60131

International Childbirth Education Association, P.O. Box 5852, Milwaukee, Wisconsin 53220

American Society for Psycho-prophylaxis in Obstetrics, Inc., 7 West 96th Street, New York, N.Y. 10025

breastfeeding. Instead, you may be able to show him what a successful nurser you can be, in spite of any minor obstacles that come your way. He will then be able to point you out to his other patients as a shining example. A pediatrician who is enthusiastic about breastfeeding will balance out an obstetrician who is indifferent to it. So choose your pediatrician before the baby is born (see page 54), and try to choose one who is interested in helping mothers who want to nurse their babies.

As you read this, you may be well along in your pregnancy—and unhappy over your relationship with your obstetrician. Changing doctors is not a decision to be lightly undertaken, but it is possible. This is your pregnancy, your labor, your birth experience, and your baby. Your first obligation is to your own physical and mental health, not to your doctor's feelings. (Besides, doctors are made of pretty durable material; they all get over having an occasional patient switch allegiance.)

CHOOSING YOUR HOSPITAL

In you live in a community where you have a choice of hospitals, you can judge them according to several criteria. The most important is accreditation. The Joint Commission on Accreditation of Hospitals, sponsored by the American Hospital Association, American Medical Association, American College of Physicians, and American College of Surgeons, has drawn up a set of standards "evolved from years of experience and observation of hospital practices that have proved to be consistent with a high quality of patient care." A hospital must meet these standards before it is accredited.

In addition, you will want to know a hospital's maternity care policies. If it offers "family-centered" maternity care, it is likely to favor those practices that make breastfeeding easier. It may offer some or all of the following: classes for prospective mothers and fathers; an invitation to see the maternity facilities ahead of time; a general policy of keeping mothers awake during delivery; permission for husbands to remain with their wives during labor and delivery; and a rooming-in plan. These services are all important, to a greater or lesser degree. The prenatal courses let the mother know what to expect during childbirth and help her prepare for it. They also help the husband feel very much a part of the coming event, and better able to provide the reassurance and help you will want. It is better if the mother is not too heavily medicated, since some of the medication given to the mother passes through the placenta to the baby, making him sleepy and uninterested in nursing for several days. However, not all women want or can have a completely unmedicated delivery. You will definitely want to discuss this aspect of delivery with your obstetrician well in advance of your due date.

The most important hospital policy as far as breastfeeding is concerned may be the rooming-in plan, a system that lets a mother keep her baby in her room for a major part of the hospital day. During the 1890s, hospitals set up central nurseries for the benefit of those few mothers who were too sick to care for their babies themselves. Eventually all babies migrated to the central nursery—until the 1940s, when rooming-in began to come back in favor. Rooming-in combines the best elements of giving birth at home with the advantages of modern obstetrical care. Rooming-in is particularly conducive to breastfeeding because the physical closeness of the mother to her baby encourages a quick response to the baby's needs, and because demand feeding, or feeding the baby when he wants to eat, is possible. When Duke Hospital in North Carolina began a compulsory rooming-in plan, the breastfeeding rate there rose from 5% to 58.5%. A description of a typical rooming-in plan is in Chapter Five.

To find out which hospitals in your area provide family-centered maternity service, including rooming-in, telephone their departments of obstetrics and gynecology or ask your local representatives of La Leche League, ICEA or ASPO (addresses on page 51).

CHOOSING A PEDIATRICIAN

It is advisable to find a pediatrician at least three months ahead of your due date. Should you deliver prematurely, you will be especially grateful to know that you can count on prompt, top-notch medical care for your baby. You can go about finding a pediatrician the same way you sought your obstetrician—through the hospital, your family doctor, your friends, or special-interest organizations. If you are particularly happy with your obstetrician, you might ask him to recommend a pediatrician.

Make an appointment to meet your prospective pediatrician before your baby is born. Tell him your due date, your hospital, and the name of your obstetrician. Agree on a procedure to let him know when your baby has arrived. (Your husband will probably be the one to make that first postnatal call to the pediatrician, along with his calls to grandparents and friends notifying them of the happy event. If he won't be able to do this, you can ask your obstetrician or a nurse at the hospital to let the pediatrician know of the baby's birth.)

When you first meet with the pediatrician, be sure to tell him that you plan to breastfeed and that you would like to have rooming-in. Ask him how many of his patients breast-feed. If he says, "Hardly any," he probably does not whole-heartedly support those who do and may suggest a switch to formula at the first cloud on the horizon. Bring up any other questions you may have, such as the advisability of circumcision for baby boys, or the age at which he customarily advises starting the feeding of solid foods. (Doctors "sold" on breastfeeding seldom start solids earlier than three months, and sometimes later.)

After speaking to the pediatrician for a while, you can probably tell whether he is the doctor for you. You may walk away thinking that he is a brilliant doctor who can give optimal care to your children if they become ill, but wish that he were a more ardent supporter of breastfeeding. In a case like this, you might want to stick with him, and discuss the value of breastfeeding. In Chapter Nine, we will talk about how to handle those situations when your doctor gives you advice that you feel will undermine the success of your breast-feeding. Many times these apparent conflicts can be worked out so that both doctor and mother end up feeling that, thanks to improved communication, they are doing the best for the baby.

NUTRITION DURING PREGNANCY AND LACTATION

"How is it that poor men's wives, who have no cold fowl and port wine on which to be coshered up, nurse their children without difficulty, whereas the wives of rich men, who eat and drink everything that is good, cannot do so, we will for the present leave to the doctors and mothers to settle between them." This paradox that puzzled the British novelist Anthony Trollope back in 1847 is still true today. How is it that poorly nourished women in famine-devastated Indian villages can produce enough milk to keep their totally breast-fed babies healthy for their first six months of life, while well-fed women in western countries often have difficulty giving enough milk even for the early weeks?

As valid as this question may be, its answer should not imply that what you eat does not matter. A severely malnourished woman may not be able to lactate successfully. And the woman who is not getting an adequate diet will produce milk only by drawing nutrients from her own body. This cannot go on indefinitely; eventually her milk yield is sure to drop and her health is sure to suffer. One Australian study found that 74% of women with good or excellent diets in their latter half of pregnancy breastfed their babies through the seventh month, while only 6% of women with very poor diets were able to breastfeed this long. This bears out the truth that, all other things being equal, the well-nourished mother will have more milk for a longer time and will feel better while nursing than the poorly nourished woman.

Ideally, of course, you should have been well nourished in

childhood and adolescence and throughout your adult life. The reason why good nutrition is especially important throughout pregnancy is because what you eat reaches your unborn baby in the form of the nutrients essential for growth and development. The first three months of pregnancy constitute the crucial period for the formation of the baby's organs; during the next three months, his body continues to grow and develop; and during the last three months of pregnancy, the baby stores up in his body his reserve supplies of the various food factors upon which he will rely for his first six months of life. For your baby's optimal development, both before and after birth, your diet should contain essential nutritional elements throughout your entire pregnancy. Your doctor may prescribe vitamins, to be taken during pregnancy and lactation. Take them—but do not assume that they replace a well-balanced diet.

If you were eating well before you became pregnant, you will have to make no changes during the first half of your pregnancy, and only small increases in food intake during the second half and during lactation. John McKigney, chief of the International Programs Staff of the United States Department of Health, Education and Welfare's Nutrition Program, has said, "Despite the rather extravagant advice on diet recommended in many obstetrical and nutritional texts, the nutrients required for lactation are usually obtained from a moderately increased intake of the woman's normal diet." However, American teenagers and young women have notoriously poor eating habits. If your normal diet involves skipping breakfast or lunch, or overloading on sweets or coffee to the exclusion of more nutritious foods, this is a good time to mend your ways. The chart on page 60 provides the ideal guidelines for sound nutrition during pregnancy and lactation. It does not lay down inflexible orders. If you're allergic to eggs, for example, go without them and substitute an ounce of meat or cheddar cheese, one-fourth cup of cottage cheese, or two tablespoons of peanut butter. If you hate milk, try to get the equivalent of at least a pint a day by using it in cooking or by eating cheese. (Cottage cheese is a good source of protein and a cheddar or other hard cheese provides both protein and calcium.) If you need to economize, substitute nonfat dry milk for liquid milk, cheaper cuts of meat, and whichever form of fruits and vegetables are cheapest—fresh, frozen, or canned.

LIQUID INTAKE

Liquids are important factors in the diet. They are especially important for the nursing mother, who loses fluid in her milk. You will probably find that you become thirstier while nursing. Pay attention to your body's demands for liquids. If you find that you never think of taking a drink, make a point of having a glass of water, milk, or fruit juice before each nursing. You can take some of your liquid in soups, but don't depend heavily on coffee or tea, since these drinks have a diuretic effect on some people—that is, they stimulate the kidneys to eliminate more fluid—and so the liquid does not stay in the system long enough.

HOW TO STAY SLIM WHILE NURSING

You don't have to gain weight while nursing. We know of one mother who lost twenty-two pounds in ten months while nursing her third baby. She did this by getting the maximum amount of nourishment from a minimum of calories. While you are breastfeeding, you will need to consume about 1,000 calories more than you did before you became pregnant, to make up for those calories that are expended to produce the milk, as well as those that leave your body through the milk. Eat these extra calories in high-protein, high food value items. If you find that you are putting on weight, there are many ways in which you can cut back on caloric intake without denying yourself or your baby the nourishment you both need.

You can, for example, substitute skim milk for whole milk; broil, boil, roast, or bake meats and potatoes instead of frying them; eat lean meats, particularly organ meats like liver, heart, and kidneys, and avoid fatty meats and fish like pork and mackerel; snack on raw vegetables or fruits instead of potato chips or cookies; eat fresh fruits rather than sweetened canned fruits; eat sparingly of high-calorie vegetables and fruits like avocados, cherries, lima beans, sweet potatoes, and corn; and stay far away from soft drinks, sugar-coated cereals, cookies, cakes, and candy.

WHAT FOODS SHOULD YOU AVOID DURING NURSING?

There is no food in your diet that is good for you but bad for your baby. If you can eat it safely, it's safe when it goes through the milk. Some foods eaten by the mother, though, do seem to affect the baby. This has never been medically proved, but it is a phenomenon seen often in a pediatrician's office. One nursing mother found that her baby got sick and crampy whenever she had eaten something containing garlic, and then she remembered that her husband suffers cramps for several days after he eats garlic. Other women find that their nursing babies sometimes suffer from gas after the mothers eat such gas-producing foods as cabbage, broccoli, or brussels sprouts. Some foods eaten in large amounts will give the milk a distinctive taste, which an occasional baby with a discriminating palate may not like. If you can establish any relationship between certain foods that you eat and reactions from your baby, it is easy enough to avoid these foods. For the most part, however, you can eat any nourishing food you want without fear that your baby will be affected.

WHAT FOODS MAKE MILK?

Virtually every culture in the world has proffered certain foods to nursing mothers, in the belief that they help to make milk. In his book, *Infant Nutrition in the Subtropics and Tropics,* Dr. D.B. Jelliffe lists some of the foods nursing mothers have been urged to eat in China: "a mixture of pork fat and red gram, cuttlefish soup, shrimps' heads in wine, and a special sweet wine made from glutinous rice, given together with the larvae of the blow-fly." Dr. Jelliffe also mentions the many herbal preparations relied on all over the world to increase a mother's milk supply, concluding that their effects are largely psychological: the mother thinks that a certain food will increase her milk supply, so she relaxes and has a good let-down reflex, and thus "proves" the value of the food.

In *The Psychology of Women,* Dr. Helene Deutsch writes about a poor, illiterate wet nurse, for whom "one of the greatest advantages of her vocation consisted in the fact that she was supposed to drink a quart of beer a day, in order to increase her secretion of milk. The favorable influence of beer on the glandular activity, which was considered an indubitable fact in former times, yielded her a pleasure prize that she turned into an obligation for her employers. One day, on the recommendation of a physician, her employers tried to give her less beer and the production of milk stopped at once. It began again when she was given the full quota of beer. So far as I can remember, at that time everyone about her was much more impressed by the miraculous virtue of the beer than by that of the nurse's defiant protest."

Psychology does affect physiology, but it is possible that the nurse's beer may actually have been beneficial. Beer that is made with brewer's yeast is particularly rich in vitamin B. And vitamin B is sometimes prescribed for general fatigue. Anything that ameliorates "that tired feeling" is bound to help a nursing mother build up her milk supply, and some form of additional vitamin B seems to work for many mothers. You can get extra vitamin B from pills, from a daily glass of beer made with brewer's yeast (usually imported beer) or from one to three teaspoons a day of dried nutritional (brewer's) yeast. This is not the same kind of yeast used in baking bread; it is sold especially as a dietary supplement and can be mixed into a glass of fruit juice.

If your milk supply is ample, don't worry about eating anything extra. If not, and if your doctor approves, you might try the additional vitamin B. Also check Chapter Six for suggestions on building up your milk supply.

THE FOODS YOU SHOULD EAT EACH DAY* FOOD ITEM	Non-Pregnant State and First Half of Pregnancy	Latter Half of Pregnancy	While Breast-feeding
Milk—may be whole, skim, evaporated, dry, or buttermilk. May be used in creamed soups or vegetables or in puddings. May substitute cheese or ice cream.	1 pint	1 quart	1 quart
Lean cooked meat, fish or poultry. Eat liver or heart often (rich in iron). May sometimes substitute dry beans or peas, lentils, nuts or peanut butter.	1 serving (2–3 ounces)	1–2 servings (5 ounces)	3 or more servings
Egg	1	1	1
Fruits and vegetables rich in vitamin A (dark green or yellow)—broccoli, carrots, greens, pumpkin, winter squash, sweet potatoes, apricots, cantaloupe.	1 serving	1 serving	1 serving
Fruits and vegetables rich in vitamin C. Good sources: grapefruit, orange or tomato (whole or juice), cantaloupe, fresh strawberries, broccoli, peppers.	1 serving or	1 serving and	1 serving and
Fair sources: other melons, asparagus, brussels sprouts, raw cabbage, greens, fresh or canned chili, potatoes cooked in jackets.	2 servings	1 serving	2 servings
Other fruits and vegetables, including potatoes	1 serving	2 servings	2 servings
Whole grain, restored or enriched cereals or breads, or other grain products like cornmeal, grits, macaroni, spaghetti, rice.	3–4 servings	3–4 servings	3–4 servings
Butter or margarine	As caloric level permits		

* This chart has been adapted from information in *Prenatal Care* (1962, reprinted 1970) and *Infant Care* (1963, reprinted 1970), both publications of the Children's Bureau of the U.S. Dept. of Health, Education, and Welfare.

DRUGS AND THE NURSING MOTHER

ALCOHOLIC DRINKS

Moderate amounts of alcohol—a couple of glasses of beer or wine, or a cocktail or two in a day—will not have any ill effects on your baby. They may even help to supply him with more milk by helping you to relax. One pediatrician we know was able to make an arrangement with the hospital to permit the husbands of nursing mothers to bring in some beer or wine, so the mother could have a drink before the 6 P.M. feeding. You may not be able to do this in your hospital, but once you get home, you can go right ahead and enjoy a relaxing cocktail. For most women, the early evening feeding is usually the lightest of the day due to maternal fatigue. A pick-me-up before dinner can pick up your baby, too, by helping your let-down reflex to work.

Very large amounts of alcohol will go through the milk and affect the baby. In *Nursing Your Baby*, Karen Pryor tells of the mother and baby who both passed out after the mother had drunk a quart of port wine at a sitting.

CIGARETTES

Nicotine passes through your milk to your baby, but most of it is altered in your baby's liver and kidney. Since gastro-intestinal absorption is slow, you would expect few if any severe toxic reactions in the nursing baby of a smoking mother. And, in fact, there is no proof of ill effects. However, since nicotine is a highly poisonous drug, you should try to stop smoking while you are nursing, or at least cut down. If giving up cigarettes makes you so tense that your milk production is affected, go back to them—but try to smoke as little as possible.

If you are pregnant now, you will be interested in the results of recent studies that found that heavy smokers tend to have smaller babies than non-smokers. On top of all the other evidence on the ill effects of smoking, this may make you decide to kick the habit for good—both for your own sake and your baby's.

MARIJUANA

The little that we know about marijuana makes us agree with the statement by Dr. Jay M. Arena, president of the American Academy of Pediatrics and director of the Poison Control Center at Duke University School of Medicine, that for the nursing mother, "marijuana smoking is courting tragedy." While we know less about marijuana than about any other intoxicant, we do know that its most active ingredient is fat-soluble and is, therefore, likely to appear in breast milk. We have no hard evidence that marijuana smoking by the mother is harmful to her baby, but it would be foolish to take chances by exposing your infant to the possibly dangerous effects of this powerful substance.

"HARD" DRUGS: LSD, HEROIN, "UPS" AND "DOWNS"

If taking marijuana while pregnant or nursing is dangerous, taking any of these hard drugs is embracing disaster. Babies born to women addicted to heroin or morphine derivatives are themselves born addicted and must be aided medically to withdraw from their dependence on the drug. We have no similar knowledge of the effects of these drugs on nursing babies—but do we really need it?

ORAL CONTRACEPTIVES

These should be avoided by the nursing mother. All of these tablets contain synthetic estrogen and/or progesterone —hormones which inhibit the production of milk. (Similar hormone preparations are commonly given to non-nursing mothers to help dry up their milk.) Even if you might turn out to be among that minority of women whose production of milk is not affected by the oral contraceptives, there is another consideration—the effects of these powerful hormones on your growing baby. We don't know yet just how much medication comes through the milk to the baby, and we have no idea of the possible long-range effects of daily doses of estrogen and progesterone on an infant's developing endocrine system.

DRUGS DURING CHILDBIRTH

We know that some of the medication given to the mother passes through the placenta to the baby. The mother's wears off in a few hours, but it may take as much as a week for all the depressant drugs to be eliminated from the baby's immature system. As a result, the baby whose mother received a great deal of analgesia and anesthesia during childbirth is likely to be quite sleepy the first few days of his life. While this may have no permanent effect on the full-size, full-term baby, it does affect all his early activities, including, of course, his interest in nursing.

Since the vigorous sucking of a hungry baby is vital for establishing an ample supply of milk in the mother, the mother of a sleepy infant who is not interested in nursing is at a definite disadvantage in building up her milk. Dr. T. Berry Brazelton, a Boston pediatrician, compared the breast-feeding responses of babies whose mothers had received the average doses of barbiturates two to eight hours before delivery, those who had had an inhalant anesthetic administered during the actual delivery and those who had received local anesthetics or no medication at all. Dr. Brazelton found that the babies of nonmedicated and locally anesthetized mothers recovered from the trauma of birth quickly and were nursing and beginning to gain weight by the third day. "But," he concluded, "babies delivered with barbiturate premedicants had weight gain delayed by twenty-four to forty-eight hours and had impaired responses to the nursing situation."

If anesthesia during childbirth is indicated, a regional anesthetic, such as a caudal or saddle block which desensitizes only the mother's pelvic region, is usually preferred over a general anesthesia which puts her to sleep. This is because medication given by regional techniques does not enter the blood stream, and therefore cannot reach the baby's system.

MEDICINES

When you are nursing a baby, you may take an occasional aspirin, anti-histamine or tablespoon of mineral oil (as a laxative) without checking first with your doctor. But you should not be taking large amounts of any of these, nor should you be taking any of them over a period of time without his knowledge. Before taking any new or unusual drug, check with your pediatrician, as well as with your own doctor. First of all, the symptoms you are trying to get rid of may be significant for your own health. And, secondly, the medicine that you take may be harmful to your baby. Some drugs pass into your milk in amounts that might affect your baby, while others may be taken with safety. The amount of a drug that you take is important. Even if only a relatively small amount of the drug reaches your baby through your milk, it may be a large amount for him. About one-twelfth of the adult dose would be a full dose for a ten-pound baby.

If you and your doctor are not sure about the safety of a particular drug, you may get some help by calling your local poison control center. One rule of thumb a doctor can follow is whether he would administer one-twelfth of the dosage of a particular drug to a baby. If not, you as a nursing mother should not be taking it.

You should not be taking large doses of any drug, or any amount of a new and unusual drug while you are breastfeeding. The following medicines are known to have undesirable effects and so should be avoided by nursing mothers: diuretics, atropine, reserpine, lithium, chloramphenicol, cortisone and its derivatives, radioactive preparations, anti-cancer agents, anticoagulants, bromides, anti-thyroid drugs, laxatives containing cascara or senna, ergot, metronidazole (Flagyl), imipramine (Tofranil), and gallium citrate (Ga 67). This is not a complete list, and since we are constantly learning about the effects of drugs, it is still important to check with your pediatrician before taking *any* medication while you are breastfeeding.

Medicines that you may be able to take in the usual doses are antibiotics, morphine, codeine, sulfa drugs, iodides, quinine, aspirin, and some tranquilizers. Large amounts of barbiturates come through the milk and can make a baby sleepy, but small amounts seem to do no harm. The diabetic mother on insulin or tolbutamide (Orinase) and the epileptic mother taking Dilantin can in almost all cases breastfeed safely; if the baby does develop any reaction to the drug, he can then be taken off the breast.

CARE OF THE BREASTS

Most women around the world don't do anything at all to prepare their breasts for nursing; yet they breastfeed successfully with hardly any problems. In our country, a number of routines are often recommended. Some of these do seem to be helpful, some actually hinder successful nursing, and some don't seem to matter much one way or the other.

Rubbing the nipples with a nail brush to toughen them, or applying alcohol, witch hazel, or tincture of benzoin to harden them both fit into the second category. These measures irritate the nipples and predispose them to cracking and pain. Do not apply any drying agent to your nipples and do not treat them harshly. In fact, during the last two or three months of pregnancy and while you are nursing, you should not even be using soap on them. The glands on and around the nipples will be secreting substances to keep them clean, so there is no need to use soap, which has a drying effect.

TOUGHENING THE NIPPLES DURING PREGNANCY

It is a good idea to try to toughen your nipples somewhat before you begin to nurse. The breasts of the average bra-wearing American woman are so well protected that the nipples are not used to any friction at all and may become quite tender when the baby starts to suck. This is particularly true of fair-complexioned blondes and redheads.

Here are several good ways to toughen your nipples, any or all of which may be started about two or three months before your due date:

- *With a rough washcloth or towel, rub the nipples briskly when you take your daily shower.*

- *For a few minutes each day, walk around the house with your breasts uncovered, to expose the nipples to the air.*
- *Allow the nipples to rub against your clothing occasionally, either by going without a bra or by cutting a little hole in your bra around the nipple area.*
- *Expose your breasts to ultra-violet rays, either in direct sunlight or from a sunlamp. Either way, take care to avoid sunburn by starting with a very brief exposure and gradually working up. If you're sunbathing outdoors, expose your breasts for five minutes the first day, ten minutes the second, fifteen minutes the third, and so forth until they are getting the sun for half an hour daily. If you use a sun lamp, time yourself very carefully. Sit four feet away, and expose your breasts for thirty seconds the first two days, one minute the next two, two minutes the next two, and three minutes every day thereafter. If your skin turns pink at any step along the way, cut back to the previous day's exposure for a while. Always cover your eyes while sunning.*
- *In his book,* Husband-Coached Childbirth, *Dr. Robert A. Bradley recommends enlisting a helper—your husband—to stimulate your breasts manually and orally. Aside from being a pleasant way to pass the time, such handling helps the breasts get into shape for the baby.*
- *Some women find it helpful to do the simple exercise of nipple rolling once or twice a day. Take the nipple between your thumb and forefinger and pull it out firmly—just enough so that you feel it but not enough so that it really hurts. Then roll the nipple between your fingers for a minute or two. Afterwards, apply a mild cream like pure lanolin, Vitamin A & D ointment, baby oil, cold cream, or cocoa butter to the areola and the sides of the nipple—but not over the duct openings.*

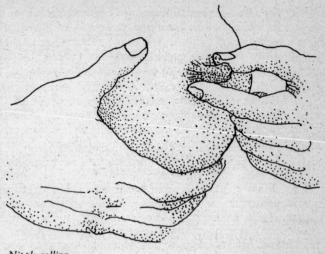

Nipple rolling

BREAST MASSAGE

Breast massage and prenatal expression of colostrum are sometimes recommended during pregnancy. They have not been proved to be of real value, but some women and doctors swear by them, so we will briefly describe them.

The purpose of breast massage is to bring the colostrum from the alveoli to the milk pools under the areolae and to stretch and prevent clogging of the milk ducts. It is also said to improve circulation and to help prevent engorgement of the breasts after birth. Dr. Robert M. Applebaum, a Florida pediatrician, advises expectant mothers to do this twice a day: circle the breast with the fingers and thumbs of both hands, and then close them together gently, first about ten times around the outer area and then about ten times midway between the outer area and the areola.

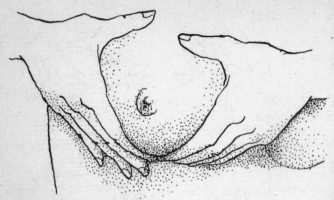

Breast massage

MANUAL EXPRESSION

Prenatal hand-expression of colostrum is also supposed to open the milk ducts and prevent engorgement, although we are not convinced that it really makes any difference. Also, since no one yet knows whether there is a fixed amount of colostrum in the breasts or whether it replaces itself, there is a possibility that this valuable substance may be wasted through hand-expression. It is a good idea, though, to learn how to express milk before your baby is born. Later on, you may want to express some milk to relieve engorgement, to supply milk if your baby is premature, or to fill a relief bottle. Since you have more time now than you will after the baby arrives, you might as well learn this technique toward the end of your pregnancy. Here's how it works:

- *Wash your hands.*
- *Hold a clean cup under your breast.*
- *Hold your breast at the edge of the areola, with your thumb above and your fingers beneath.*
- *Push your thumb and fingers together, back toward the chest wall.*
- *Do this at several different spots around the areola.*

During pregnancy, you'll only get a drop or two of colostrum.

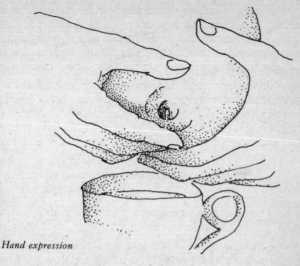

Hand expression

After your milk supply is established, you should be able to express several ounces of milk at a time.

STRETCH MARKS

Women often associate "stretch marks," whitish streaks that appear on the breasts of some mothers, with breastfeeding. Actually, like the similar lines that appear on the abdomens of some women, they result from the stretching of the skin during pregnancy. There is no known method of avoiding them, and so if you develop them, you might as well, as Dr. Bradley advises, wear them proudly as the "'service stripes' of motherhood."

INVERTED NIPPLES

Some women have nipples that seem flat or folded in but that will actually function quite well when the time comes. To determine whether your nipples are inverted, perform this little test: hold your breast at the edge of the areola between your thumb and forefinger and squeeze gently. If the nipple seems to disappear within the flesh of the breast, it is inverted. Usually nipples like this protrude normally by the end of pregnancy, and in almost all cases they come out fully when the baby starts to nurse. Occasionally, however, they remain inverted and pose a real problem to the baby who cannot grasp the breast. Fortunately, such a condition is almost always correctible.

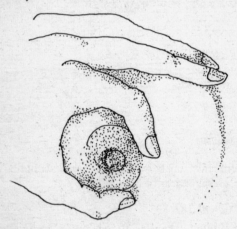

One exercise that sometimes helps involves grasping the nipple between your thumb and forefinger, drawing it forward and holding it there for a few seconds. This should be done twice a day. Another measure that sometimes brings out inverted nipples involves applying suction with a small hand-operated breast pump.

The most successful treatment, however, is the wearing of special plastic breast shields during pregnancy. These Woolwich shields are not the same type of shields sometimes recommended for use later in nursing. In fact, they cannot be used after the baby is born, since they trap droplets of milk, retaining the moisture and causing sore nipples. Originally designed to protect the clothes of nursing mothers, the Woolwich shields were adapted for their present use by an English obstetrician. They fit inside the bra and have an opening in their base into which the nipple is eventually drawn. They are worn for only a couple of hours at first; then the time is gradually extended until they are in place all day, or in severe cases all day and night. They are comfortable and inconspicuous. Ask your obstetrician whether you should use these shields. He may be able to get them for you; if not, you can obtain them for $2.75 a pair from La Leche League, 9616 Minneapolis Avenue, Franklin Park, Illinois 60131.

WEARING THE RIGHT BRASSIERE

Since your breasts will be expanding during pregnancy, you will have to get larger bras sometime around your fifth month. By your eighth month, your breasts will most likely have grown as large as they are going to be, even during the nursing period, so if you want to get a couple of nursing bras at this time, you should feel fairly safe about having the right size. Nursing bras greatly simplify the life of the breastfeeding mother; they have a row of hooks down the front, or a hook at the top of each cup, so that you may uncover one breast at a time without taking off your bra. Some hospitals supply halter-type garments which you may want to wear instead of your own bras. Your own are more attractive—but the hospital will launder its own supplies. So the choice of beauty or convenience is up to you.

Many nursing bras have a plastic lining to protect your clothes from leaking milk. Some of these are removable and can be easily changed. If not, and if you have sensitive skin, snip out the plastic lining at once; it traps moisture around the nipple, causing soreness. If your skin is fairly hardy you might try the liner since it is a great convenience, but be prepared to remove it at the first sign of sore nipples. See Chapter Six for other ways to deal with the problem of leaking milk.

A properly fitted bra is important in maintaining your breast contours, so keep the following points in mind when you go shopping. The cup of the bra should support the entire lower half of the breast in a natural position. (With the bra on, hold your arms straight down at your sides; if it fits properly, the nipple line will be level with a point midway between elbow and shoulder.) The band should fit snugly, neither binding nor slipping up or down. To test this, put your hands on your hips and look at yourself, front and back, in the mirror. The straps should be broad and adjustable. The bra should not be so tight that it leaves marks in your skin either under the arms, under the breasts or over your shoulders.

CARE OF THE BREASTS WHILE NURSING

Every hospital seems to have its own favorite routine for nipple care. If yours is clinging to such outmoded ideas as washing the nipples with soap or other drying agents, you can probably figure out a way not to follow orders. If the hospital nurse asks you to wash your nipples with sterile water before each feeding, go ahead and do it. It's not necessary, but it doesn't have any ill effects.

When you come home, you can dispense with any special nipple-care rituals. Be especially careful not to use any drying agents on your nipples—including soap. If you splash water over the nipples during your daily shower and change your bra at least once a day (or more often, if you are leaking a lot of milk), your nipples will be clean.

If you are a fair-skinned blonde or readhead with especially sensitive skin, you may want to apply a soothing ointment like plain unmedicated lanolin to your nipples after each feeding. This preparation should be wiped off before the baby nurses.

Most women experience a little bit of soreness, usually on the second or third day of nursing, but occasionally later. If you develop soreness that is more than mildly uncomfortable and if it does not go away in a day or two, treat it immediately, as suggested in Chapter Nine, pages 148–149.

THE NEED FOR ADEQUATE REST

Every new mother tires easily due to her added responsibilities and her subtracted hours of sleep. You owe it to yourself and your baby to get enough rest so that you will be able to keep your health and meet your baby's needs. As a nursing mother, this is particularly important, since your production of milk is closely linked to your physical condition. Also, if you are rundown, you are more susceptible to infections which can make nursing painful and distressing.

You may be considering hiring a baby nurse to help you when you bring the baby home from the hospital. If you know a warm, motherly nurse who loves babies and breastfeeding mothers, and who likes to cook for the whole family and do light housekeeping as well, you are unbelievably lucky. Such gems are rare indeed. The more typical baby nurse may love babies but is noticeably cool toward mothers, especially toward that queer variety who think they can feed their babies themselves, without any help from a bottle-bearing nurse. Her coolness also may extend toward doing any work in the home that is not directly related to the care of the new baby. Such a nurse is not only apt to be of little help; she is almost certain to sabotage your breastfeeding regime. At the first sign of fussiness in the baby, she will blame your milk. So if you can't find a gem of a baby nurse, don't hire any at all.

You may be lucky enough to find someone—maybe even a high school girl—who can come in for a few hours each afternoon, straighten up the house a little bit, take your older children out for a walk, and cook and clean up after dinner. If your budget can possibly be stretched to allow for this kind of help for a few weeks, you'll find it a wonderful investment.

If hired help is out of the question and if your husband's schedule does not permit him to perform many housekeeping chores, you'll just have to learn to shut your eyes to a few things for a while—to those dust balls under the living-room couch, the wrinkles in your toddler's unironed overalls, and the packages of prepared food temporarily replacing your good home cooking. It is far more important for you to get enough rest than it is to be the best housekeeper on the block. You or your husband can always catch up with your housework in a few weeks, but these first days and weeks at home are a crucial period for the nursing couple. If you over-tire yourself now, you may undermine your breastfeeding success. Obviously, you can't let everything go. You all have to eat, you all need clean clothes, and you don't want to live in chaos. For suggestions on how your husband and your older children can help you, see Chapters Six and Seven. For the present, though, you can best ensure good care and feeding for your baby by being sure that you get good care, feeding, and rest yourself.

CHAPTER 5.

NURSING BEGINS

There he is—that squalling, squirming, red-faced mite of humanity whose arrival has been so eagerly awaited all these months. You marvel at the wonder of his tiny fingers and toes. You are amazed to realize that this small person actually grew in your body. You draw him close to you, to cuddle him and love him.

And then the questions begin to rush through your mind. How will you be able to care for such a dependent little creature? How will you know what to do—and when and how to do it? It may buoy up your confidence to stop a minute and consider that women have been having first babies for thousands of years, and somehow have coped well enough so that each succeeding generation has survived to bear its own progeny.

Like every other new mother, you are apt to have questions about every aspect of child care, not the least of which involve feeding your baby. In this chapter, we will talk about those questions that inevitably come up right after the baby arrives, when you and he are still in the hospital.

HOW DOES NURSING FIT IN WITH HOSPITAL ROUTINES?

In their earnest concern for a germ-free environment and in their chronically under-staffed state, hospitals sometimes impose restrictions that are extremely inconvenient for individual patients. This is particularly true in the case of the nursing couple. Hospital regulations that may prevent a healthy mother from seeing her infant for many hours after birth, that require each baby to be on a strict four-hour feeding schedule, and that rigidly limit the length of individual feeding sessions seem designed to thwart successful breastfeeding.

An increasing number of hospital administrators, however, are coming to realize that the optimum physical and emotional health of mothers and infants sometimes demands certain changes in traditional hospital procedure. As a result, more and more hospitals are instituting the policy of rooming-in. Usually, this is in effect from early morning until the mother goes to sleep, when the infant is taken back to the nursery. Other hospitals leave mother and baby together twenty-four hours a day. And some give the mother a choice as to whether she wants full or partial rooming-in, or no rooming-in at all.

If you are lucky enough to have rooming-in, your first few days of nursing should be much easier. For only through living with your baby can you adjust your milk supply to his needs. Too often in the traditional hospital set-up, an infant wakes up in the nursery, screaming with hunger an hour or two before his scheduled feeding. The nurses try to comfort him, to no avail. Finally, the baby exhausts himself with his crying and sinks into a deep sleep—just at the time that he is due to be wheeled in to his mother. She eagerly tries to nurse him, but he is fast asleep. Despite all her attempts to rouse him, he snoozes on through the "feeding" session. An hour later, he wakes up—and is again forced to wait. This cycle may repeat itself for several feedings. Needless to say, it is frustrating for both mother and baby, and the complete antithesis to the ideal situation which can be realized only when mother and child have complete access to each other all day long.

If you are in a rooming-in unit, your baby's routine may be something like this. Immediately after birth, he may be taken to a special nursery just for rooming-in babies, where he will remain until he is examined by the pediatrician, usually within twelve hours of birth. His first two feedings may consist of plain water. By giving the baby only water at first, the doctors can satisfy themselves that he can swallow normally and will be able to handle the milk. At the next regularly scheduled daytime feeding, your baby will be brought to you to stay in your room day and night, or perhaps only until after the 10 P.M. feeding, when he will go back to the nursery.

He will sleep in a rolling crib, designed so that you can reach both baby and his supplies without getting out of bed. Your room, which may accommodate from one to four mothers and babies, will be equipped like the central nursery, complete with foot pedals for laundry hampers and antibacterial soap. Everyone who comes into your room while your baby is there will wear a special hospital gown.

On your first day of rooming-in, a nurse will show you all the baby-care equipment and supplies in the room. She will also help you put your baby to the breast, teach you how to change his diapers, and bathe and dress him. She will also show you how to keep written records of your baby's feeding and elimination patterns. After the nurse has demonstrated all of this and answered your questions, she will leave your baby with you. Your first thoughts may be, "What did I let myself in for? How can I possibly remember everything?" It is reassuring to know that you can always ring for the nurse to ask for help, or if you are not feeling well, to take the baby back to the nursery. Your rest is not likely to be overly disturbed, since healthy newborns usually sleep most of the time.

When you do hear your baby cry, you will take him from his crib and put him to your breast. After he has finished nursing, you will put him back to bed. He will probably nurse about every two-and-a-half or three hours although he may want to feed more often. Since his hunger for food and for your comforting arms will be satisfied immediately, he will sleep better and will eventually work out his own schedule. At the same time, the frequent sucking will stimulate your breasts to produce more milk, helping you to establish an ample milk supply within a couple of days. Since your breasts will be emptied often, they will not become engorged and uncomfortable.

Usually special evening visiting hours are set aside for

fathers only. This is your husband's chance to learn how to diaper and burp his baby. Some hospitals also permit other visitors in the afternoon, requiring the baby to be back in the nursery during these visiting hours. If the visiting session is a long one, say three hours, this virtually eliminates the possibility of real demand feeding. For if the baby is not fed right before visiting time, he is apt to become extremely hungry before he can come back to you. If you have a choice between a hospital that permits liberal visiting privileges and one that is strict in deference to the requirements of demand feeding, take the stricter one. The advantages of demand feeding far outweigh the pleasant opportunity to see your friends and relatives during the few days you are in the hospital.

Aside from its advantages to the nursing couple, rooming-in offers other benefits. It gives the new mother and father a chance to become acquainted with their baby and to get used to his natural eating and sleeping rhythms. It also accustoms the baby to the ordinary noises of conversation and people's comings and goings, helps to prevent the spread of infection by separating him from the other newborn infants, and most important, restores the baby to his rightful place by his mother's side. After you have carried a baby under your heart for nine months, it seems cruel and strange to whisk him away from you immediately after birth. A baby needs more from his mother than a feeding every four hours—and you need more from him.

While the trend among hospitals is in the direction of providing more opportunities for rooming-in, most hospitals still do not have it. If you can get it, you're lucky. If not, don't despair. Human beings are adaptable creatures, and most mothers and babies are able to make their necessary temporary adjustments to the rigid schedules of the average hospital.

If you don't have rooming-in, ask your obstetrician or your pediatrician to request that your baby be brought to you on a three-hour schedule rather than the usual four-hour one, in recognition of the fact that the breastfed baby usually eats more frequently than the bottle-fed infant. You may also ask your doctor to leave instructions that your baby receive no bottles at all in the nursery (except for those first two bottles of water), since the relative ease of drinking from a rubber nipple may discourage him from putting out the extra effort needed to suck vigorously at the breast.

Your doctor may, however, be unable to accomplish any change in hospital routines, or, for one reason or another, he may consider it unwise to do so. Your hospital may insist on four-hour feeding schedules, on feeding breastfed babies bottles of water for the entire first day, and on taking them back to the nursery at the moment feeding time is officially over.

If you had an easy delivery, if your baby is a good size, and if you have someone to help you at home, one way of circumventing extremely strict hospital rules is to ask your doctor whether you can go home a day or two early. He may feel that this would be possible, even advisable. On the other hand, he may have some sound reasons why he feels you should stay the full time (usually only four or five days).

Even if you feel that hospital procedures are interfering with your relationship with your baby, take heart. You will be within these sterile walls only a few days. Many other women have borne babies in similar circumstances and gone on to nurse them successfully. Finally, you really do agree with the hospital's principal concern: sending home as many healthy mothers and babies as possible.

PKU TESTING

Many hospitals routinely test all newborns for phenylketonuria, or PKU. Even though this is a very rare disease, widespread testing is justified by the fact that the harmful effects of the disease will be completely offset if the affected child receives a special diet from his first few days of life.

Some hospitals want all new breastfed infants to receive

one or more bottles of formula for the purposes of the PKU test, so that the babies' urine can reach a high protein level earlier than if they were totally breastfed. This is not necessary. The PKU test—which is run on the blood more often than on the urine in newborns—can be performed just as easily on wholly breastfed babies as on bottle-fed babies. By the optimum time for administering the test—between the fourth and seventh day of life—the blood of every baby, whether breastfed or bottle-fed, can be analyzed for the presence or absence of PKU. *It is, therefore, not necessary to give your baby formula for the purpose of the PKU test.*

SPEAK UP IN THE HOSPITAL

No matter how excellent your hospital care may be, you have to remember that you are only one patient among many. Doctors and nurses have other things on their minds; they may not always be as closely attuned to your wishes as you would like. As a breastfeeding mother, you will want certain things done certain ways. Don't be shy about asking or reminding your doctor and nurses about these aspects of care for you and your baby. If you are polite and pleasant, no one is likely to take offense. These are some points you may want to bring up:

- *When you first go into the hospital, remind your doctor and any nurses who come around to give you medicine, that you are planning to breastfeed and should not, therefore, receive any drugs to dry up your milk. (If by mistake you have received some, don't worry. Putting your baby to the breast will still bring in the milk.)*

- *Some hospitals automatically feed all babies in the nursery at 2 A.M. and 6 A.M. At the first 10 P.M. feeding, ask the nurse to be sure to bring your baby in to you at all regularly scheduled feedings. Your breasts need the stimulation, and he should receive your milk, not a bottle of formula.*

- *If you are shy about breastfeeding in front of your roommate, ask the nurse to put a screen around your bed.*
- *If your breasts are filling up uncomfortably between feedings, tell your doctor and nurse. The hospital may have an electric breast pump that you can use to relieve the fullness. See "Expressing and Storing Milk," Chapter Nine. Or the nurse may be able to help you express some of your milk by hand into a glass or cup. (If the nurse doesn't know how, follow the instructions for hand-expression given in Chapter Four.)*
- *If you're uncomfortable for any reason at all, tell your doctor and nurse. They will probably be able to do something to alleviate your discomfort.*

HOW SOON SHOULD THE NEWBORN BEGIN TO NURSE?

The new mother may wonder when she should first offer her breast to her baby. Knowing that the milk does not come in immediately after delivery, a thoughtful woman may fear that her infant will suffer frustration from suckling at the milk-less breast. A woman who has just had her first baby will usually have milk for him between forty-eight and seventy-two hours after delivery; if she has previously borne children, her milk will come in sooner, between thirty-six to forty-eight hours after birth. The milk comes in even earlier for some women.

Even though the breast does not have milk right away, it has, from the last weeks of pregnancy, had a rich supply of colostrum, that sweet yellowish fluid that provides such a good start to an infant's life. (See Chapter Three for a description of this wonderful first food.)

While the baby is getting the benefits of colostrum, he is also guaranteeing himself a full larder for the future; for the best way to produce an abundant milk supply is to allow a hungry infant to suck vigorously and frequently soon after birth. The more he sucks, the more milk you will produce for him.

As in so many cases, the most natural thing is the best thing. For you, the mother, the most natural time to offer your breast to your baby will be the first time you see him, as soon after birth as possible. The exact time for this first visit will vary, depending largely on how you are feeling and what the policy is at your hospital. If you were awake during the delivery in a hospital that encourages prepared childbirth, you may be permitted to hold your baby moments after he emerges from the womb. Sometimes, in fact, the obstetrician will gently place the newborn on the mother's stomach for an instant as she lies on the delivery table, even before the umbilical cord is cut. And in a few minutes, after the baby has been washed off, the mother may be able to put him briefly to the breast. Since stimulation of the breasts causes the uterus to contract, the baby's immediate suckling can speed delivery of the placenta. The contractions of the uterus also shut off the maternal blood vessels that formerly fed the baby, and therefore help to discourage excessive bleeding. In most hospitals, however, the mother may glimpse her baby momentarily right after birth, but will not have an opportunity to hold him until several hours later.

If you are fortunate enough to be in a hospital where the nurses encourage breastfeeding mothers, one of them will help you when she brings your baby to you for the first time. Do not hesitate to ask her questions; chances are, she will have heard the same queries many times before and will be able to give you sound advice. Sometimes, however, the nurses may be too rushed to give you much time—or, as willing as they may be to help you, they may not know any more than you do. If this is your situation, don't despair. There is little danger of making big mistakes in such a natural endeavor. It may take you and your baby a little longer to get the hang of things, but you both have plenty of time to get used to each other.

Just remember that you are starting off with two big

advantages. You have something that your baby wants, and he is born with the sucking urge that will help him get it. This urge to suck is so strong in some babies that they suck their thumbs while they are still in the uterus. Imagine what they will do when they can get something good to eat, along with the blissful pleasures of sucking!

PUTTING THE BABY TO THE BREAST

The first time your baby is brought to you, he may not exhibit a great urge to nurse. He may be too sleepy to be interested in anything. This is especially common in babies whose mothers received a large amount of anesthesia during delivery. Even if the baby does seem drowsy, however, it does no harm to offer him the breast. He may suck in his sleep, or he may enjoy the experience so much that he decides it's worth waking up for. If you can't manage to interest him in dinner (or breakfast or lunch), don't worry.

Many babies do not nurse well at all for their first few days. One study of 600 newborn infants found that 40% of them had to be actively helped to suck. So if your baby has trouble nursing at first, don't worry. The normal full-term infant is born with enough reserves to keep him healthy, even if he goes without eating anything for two or three days. Aside from the colostrum, the first few feeding sessions are actually more for education—yours and your baby's—than for nourishment. In fact, some English doctors call these early feedings "practice feeds." During this period, while your milk supply is becoming established, you learn how to feed your baby, and he learns how to suckle. Of course, it's easier for both parties if your baby is an eager pupil; he'll learn more quickly how to go about his tasty task. But if he isn't—if he's sleepy or if he has trouble getting the nipple in his mouth the right way, or if he keeps letting go of it—don't worry. He'll be extra-hungry before long. Meanwhile, you can use your first few visits for such important activities as feeling his downy-soft hair, inspecting his toes and getting used to the feeling of being a mother.

Even if your baby comes to you wildly hungry and eager to eat, he will probably need some help from you in mastering the feat of finding the breast. You can help in two ways: first, by making things as comfortable as possible for yourself and your baby, and secondly, by helping him locate the nipple.

You can nurse comfortably either lying down or sitting up. Which of these positions you choose depends on your own individual preference, on how you are feeling, and on what time of day it is. During the first few days after birth and for night feedings afterwards, many mothers find it more restful to lie down. Other women feel more comfortable sitting up for every feeding.

When you are lying down, it will be easiest to nurse if you lie on your side with one or two pillows behind your back and one or two under your head. A flat pillow (made of folded diapers, a receiving blanket, or a towel) placed under

Lying down while nursing

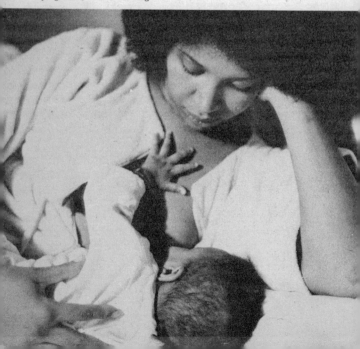

the baby's head as he lies facing you will put his mouth at breast level and make it easier for him to reach the nipple.

The sitting position seems to be more popular with most women. For maximum comfort, sit up straight in bed, with your back and head supported by one or more big pillows. Put the baby on a pillow on your lap. Bend your knees to bring him closer to your body and lean forward a little to make it easier for him to grasp the nipple.

Once you have nursed your baby a few times, you will find your own most comfortable position. When you are out of bed, you will no doubt gravitate toward a favorite seat in your home—a comfortable armchair or the corner of the couch. One young mother we know feels that her couch, which has movable arm rests, was created especially for nursing. And for hundreds of years, women have found the rhythm of a rocking chair comforting to them and their babies.

Now you and the baby are both comfortable, and it is time to "plug him in," as one five-year-old said of his baby brother. For the first couple of times, you may have to help your baby find the breast. Take advantage of his instinctive "rooting reflex," which leads the infant to turn his mouth

Compressing the breast

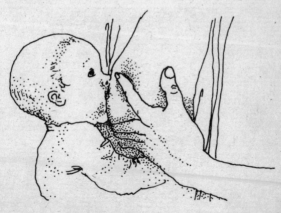

toward anything that resembles a nipple. Help him root around for the nipple by holding him against you so that the corner of his mouth touches your nipple, or by stroking one of his cheeks with the nipple until he turns his mouth to it. When he opens his mouth, gently bring him closer.

It is very important that the baby take the entire areola into his mouth, since, as we explained in Chapter Three, suckling at the breast is not real sucking, but would better be described as "gumming" or "jawing." It is the up-and-down pressure of the infant's jaws on the areola that makes the ducts release the milk. You can help your baby get hold of the nipple and areola by compressing your breast with two fingers, or a finger and thumb.

If your baby takes only the nipple into his mouth, take him off the breast (see next section on how to do this) and start over again. Try "teasing" his mouth open by lightly touching his lips with the nipple, from the upper to the lower lip and back again until he opens his mouth wide enough to accommodate nipple and areola. Let him grab for the nipple; don't just stuff it into his mouth.

Do *not* attempt to open the baby's mouth by pressing in on

Keeping the breast away from the baby's nose

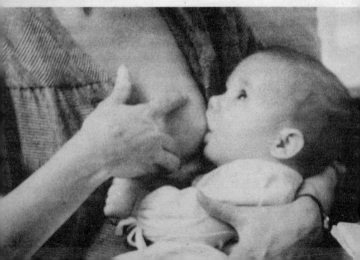

both his cheeks. He naturally tends to turn toward the side being touched; if both are touched at once, he will become confused and move his mouth frantically from side to side. Do *not* introduce your baby to nursing by pushing his head onto the breast. He may become frightened as his nose is pushed into the flesh and is more likely to wail his frustration than to seize the opportunity to nurse.

If your breasts are especially large or engorged, you may have to press your finger on the breast, to keep it away from the baby's nose. (In the event that the breast is so engorged that the baby can't get a good grip, express a little milk by hand and then bring him back to the breast.) Another trick for keeping his nasal passage free is to pull his legs close to you, so that his body will naturally be at the correct angle. It is absolutely essential to see that your baby can always breathe through his nose, since an infant *has* to breathe this way. He will not open his mouth to breathe unless he is forced to. (This is why babies have so much distress when they have a cold.)

TAKING THE BABY OFF THE BREAST

When it is time for the baby to stop nursing, insert your finger in the side of his mouth to break the suction between his mouth and your breast. Do not try to pull him off the nipple because he will automatically tighten his mouth. This can be quite painful and can contribute toward sore nipples.

ONE BREAST OR TWO?

You will probably want to offer both breasts at each feeding. This will give more milk to your baby, will better stimulate your production of milk and will help to prevent engorgement. Since the first breast is usually emptied more completely, you should alternate first choice at each feeding, starting on the side that was suckled last at the previous feeding. Keep track of first and second servings by pinning a safety pin to your bra on the side that has been offered first; switch the pin at every feeding. Don't take the baby away from the first breast while he is actively nursing. Wait until he stops to rest; then make the change.

HOW LONG SHOULD EARLY NURSING PERIODS LAST?

Doctors used to advise new mothers to nurse their babies for only one minute on each breast at each feeding for the first day of nursing; two minutes on the second day; three minutes on the third and so on until a maximum of ten minutes per breast per feeding was reached. This advice was given principally to prevent sore nipples. The only trouble was that it didn't work. Many women still got sore nipples— even though they may have first felt the tenderness two or three days later than they otherwise would have. The big problem with such short nursing periods is that they prevent the let-down reflex from working properly. It often takes a few minutes of nursing for the let-down reflex of a brand-new mother to take effect. Taking the baby from the breast before the milk lets down is frustrating to him—and also to the mother, since she is left with her breasts full of milk, a situation that may lead to painful engorgement, clogged ducts, or infection.

The other extreme—unlimited sucking right from birth— works well for some women with hardy skin, but may be a bit much for the average woman. The schedule that seems to work the best for most new mothers involves letting the baby suck for five minutes from each breast at each feeding for the first day; ten minutes for the next day; and fifteen minutes or as long as the baby wants to thereafter. Once your milk supply is well established, your let-down is functioning well, and your baby is experienced at sucking, he will get most of the milk from each breast in the first five minutes. As long as he's actively nursing, he will continue to get a little trickle, but the real appeal of the longer nursing period will be the satisfaction of his need to suck and to be held in the warmth of your arms.

Burping with baby in upright position

Burping with baby seated

Burping with baby on his stomach

BURPING THE BABY

Sometimes babies swallow a little air during a feeding. If they can bring this up in the form of a hearty burp, they will be more comfortable and ready to eat some more. Breastfed babies usually swallow less air than do bottle-fed infants, and some breastfed babies hardly ever burp after a feeding. Others invariably do, often bringing up a little milk in the process. Either way is normal.

The best time to burp your baby is after he has finished drinking from one breast. Then you can diaper him and put him to the other breast and let him drift right off to sleep as he finishes nursing. There are three common ways to burp a baby. You can hold him vertically with his head over your shoulder, sit him on your lap with one hand supporting his head, or lay him on his stomach over your knees. Put a diaper in front of him to catch any spit-up milk and then gently rub or pat his back. Please don't pound him hard! He won't like it and he won't bring up his burps any faster from being thumped. If he hasn't burped in a few minutes, don't worry about it. Go ahead and give him the other breast, and when he has finished his feeding, lay him down on his stomach or his side, so that he will easily be able to bring up any air that may still be in his stomach.

BOWEL MOVEMENTS

While your baby is still cradled in your womb, his bodily organs start to function. At about the sixth month of fetal life, a mass of cast-off cells from his liver, pancreas, and gall bladder begins to form in his intestines and remains there until birth. This dark-green tar-like substance called meconium is eliminated in his bowel movements during the first couple of days after birth. Its elimination seems to be facilitated by the colostrum from your newly lactating breasts. Once the meconium has been eliminated, your baby's stools will range in color from a golden daffodil yellow to a yellow-green to a brownish tint. The bowel movements of a breastfed baby are usually quite different from those of a bottle-fed baby. So don't worry if your baby's bowel movements are looser and more frequent than those of your room-mate's formula-fed infant.

WEIGHT LOSS AFTER BIRTH

All newborn babies lose weight after birth, mostly because of their elimination of birth fluids and meconium. A loss of up to 10% of birth weight is common, although some healthy babies may even lose a little bit more than that. Your breastfed baby will most likely take a little longer to regain his birth weight than the baby who is fed formula right from birth, but this is nothing to worry about.

AFTERPAINS

During these early breastfeeding sessions, you will probably feel abdominal pains similar to menstrual cramps. They may be very mild or surprisingly strong. The pains are apt to be stronger if this is not your first delivery. Be happy when you feel them, because they tell you that your uterus is contracting well, and they're a good sign that your let-down reflex is beginning to operate. If you are really uncomfortable, let your doctor know; perhaps he'll prescribe a mild pain reliever. In any case, these pains are short-lived; though your uterus will continue to shrink for about six weeks, you will be aware of the contractions for only the first few days after childbirth.

THOSE "BABY BLUES"

You may look at your baby sometimes, perhaps when you have just been roused from a deep sleep, and think, "motherhood is not all it's been cracked up to be," If you do, you are not alone. Practically every mother alive has at one time or another resented having to care for her baby. For no matter how you longed to have a child, and how much you love him, you now have to make scores of domestic adjustments. The new responsibilities of motherhood are sure to evoke mixed emotions. You love your baby, yet at the same time you chafe at his complete dependence upon you. And then you are overwhelmed by guilt, because you *know* mothers are supposed to love their babies *all* the time—twenty-four hours a day, seven days a week.

You may find that you are a terrible patient in the hospital —apt to fly off the handle or cry at the slightest provocation. Or you may be euphoric in the hospital but edgy when you get home, or when your mother goes back to her own home, or when your husband goes back to work. Some students of this not uncommon state of events known as "post-partum blues," blame it on the changed hormonal balance in the body of the woman who has just had a baby. There may be some truth to this, but it seems just as likely that such an emotional state is a very real reaction to the changed circumstances of your life.

If this is your first baby, you must change the entire rhythm of your life to fit the baby's. Both you and your husband are suddenly catapulted into a position of awesome responsibility. Even if you already have other children, the arrival of a new baby means that you have to rearrange the living patterns you have worked out for yourself up till now, even including the routines of caring for your older children. On top of that, you are probably wondering how you can best help your new baby's brothers and sisters happily welcome him into the family. All this when your sleep is constantly being interrupted and your body is working overtime to recover from the labor (a well-conceived term, if there ever was one) of childbirth.

Furthermore, in our society, the typical new mother tends to lack self-confidence in her maternal ability. You know motherhood must be difficult, because there are so many books telling you how to feed your children, how to handle their psyches, how to raise their IQs—even how to feed them at your breast! And if the "experts" disagree about the best theories of child-rearing, how are you to have confidence that you know what's best?

As a breastfeeding mother, your confidence may be further undermined by the fact that you are personally supplying your baby's food. When a bottle-fed baby cries—or has frequent or sparse bowel movements, or sleeps too little or too much—his mother will blame the formula, or just think that she has herself a fussy baby. In our society, the breastfeeding mother's first reaction is usually to blame herself. You worry that the baby's not getting enough milk, or that your milk isn't good enough for him, or that you're not feeding him the right way. No wonder your confidence is shaky and your feelings sometimes run away with you!

First, be reassured that by breastfeeding your baby, you are doing your best for him. Then accept your negative feelings along with the positive and realize that you are not a bad mother for having them. Not all women, of course, become emotional after the birth of a baby, but enough do so that it is not an abnormal situation. There is no need to feel guilty; we can't help how we feel about things, even though we can control what we do about our feelings. You will learn to live with these mixed feelings, as you learn to live with mixed feelings about every other aspect of life—your marriage, your job, your schooling. So it is with parenthood. We learn to take the bad with the good: the dirty diapers with the joyous gurgles, the waking up at three in the morning with the rewarding bright smile that greets us from the crib, the burdens of responsibility with the all-embracing love of a child. And when you come right down to it, most parents would agree that the joys of parenthood far outweigh its demands.

CHAPTER 6.

YOU ARE A NURSING COUPLE

GOING HOME

When you take your baby home from the hospital, you really begin to feel like a mother. You don't have to be separated from your child; you don't have to feed him according to a schedule established by someone else; you don't have to be awed by crowds of efficient people who seem to know so much more about taking care of your infant than you do. Your husband, too, begins to feel like a father. He doesn't have to be a visitor any longer to his wife and child, doesn't have to peer at his baby through a glass wall. For taking care of a baby and feeling like a family, there's no place like home.

This is not to say that these first weeks at home are easy ones. In fact, with a nursing baby, these first couple of weeks are likely to be the hardest. The baby is still a raw beginner at nursing, and so are you. Your milk has barely come in and you and your baby are still learning how best to live with each other. In addition, being at home provides its own pressures. You may return from the hospital to find dirty dishes overflowing the kitchen sink and dirty clothes erupting from the laundry hamper. If you have other children, you want to reach out and do things for them, too. In the face of the mothering you want to give them, the company you want to offer your husband, and the housework that is staring you in the face, remember one thing. These first few weeks at home are crucial ones for the nursing couple. While you don't want to—and you don't have to—shut out the rest of your family, you have to put yourself and your new baby first for a little while. You have to rest so that you can make milk; you have to feed your baby when he is hungry; you have to work at becoming a twosome.

Probably the first thing you will want to do after you have arrived home, greeted your other children, and climbed into bed will be to feed your baby. You may find that the comfort of being in your own home helps your let-down reflex to work better, and you seem to have more milk than you did in the hospital. Or the tiring trip home and the change of scene may have taken their toll by temporarily decreasing your milk supply. If this has happened, don't worry. As you rest and as your baby stimulates your breasts through frequent feedings, your milk will return. While the supply is temporarily diminished, all you have to do is nurse your baby more often. (See the next section, "How Often Should You Nurse?")

A nurse at the hospital will most likely have pressed a sealed bottle of formula into your hands, despite your insistence that you are breastfeeding. Take it home, put it on the shelf and consider it your insurance. It's also a good idea to pick up one package of six four-ounce bottles of prepared formula, to keep in the house for emergency use. Under ordinary circumstances, you won't give your new baby a bottle of formula. He has you; he doesn't need the bottle. If you are too quick to give him milk from a bottle, he will come to prefer this.

But—and this is a big but—you will have more peace of mind if you know that, should anything happen to interfere with breastfeeding your baby at his usual time, he will not have to scream with hunger. Usually, nothing will happen. But there are those rare occasions when a mother becomes ill, develops fever, diarrhea, or vomiting, and feels so washed-out that she feels she has to skip a feeding. Or you may dash out for what you think is a quick shopping trip, get caught in traffic and not get home till past the baby's feeding time. If situations like these should come up, you will know that whoever is staying with the baby can easily give him a bottle. And you will have the peace of mind that comes from being well-insured against any contingency. You may never use the formula for the baby. If you don't, we hear it makes awfully good pancakes!

In any case, remember—this pantry shelf supply should not be used in the first month except for emergencies. The human animal is lazy. We all like to do whatever is easiest, and sucking from a bottle is so much easier than milking a mother's breast that many a baby who is freely given bottles of formula in his early days decides that this easy life is for him.

HOW OFTEN SHOULD YOU NURSE?

Among many peoples around the world, nursing is very simple. The mother is next to her baby all the time; he sleeps in her room with her, and when she is up and about he rides in a sling on her side or back. As soon as the baby begins to whimper, she puts him to the breast. He nurses for a while and then drops off to sleep. When he awakes soon again and begins to make noises, she offers him the other breast. This way, the infant is almost constantly being offered food and comfort, and the mother's breasts are almost constantly being stimulated. This is true demand feeding.

Earlier in this century, as a natural outgrowth of the American love for timetables and efficiency, physicians became convinced that the best way to feed an infant was to establish a strict schedule—one feeding every four hours, or, occasionally, every three hours. This established schedule was never to be departed from.

Today, few women would be interested in either one of these extremes. As much as they love their new babies, they would probably find it too demanding to breastfeed their babies whenever they whimpered. Yet the other extreme of letting an unhappy baby wail and scream because the minute hand on his mother's watch hasn't caught up with his stomach is abhorrent to them. The schedule that seems to suit most modern mothers and babies is termed "modified demand."

Think what you want to accomplish in caring for your

baby. You want him to be happy and content with life. You want to satisfy his hunger for food and his longings to be held and cuddled. You want him to realize that he has the power to influence his world. By answering his needs as well as you can when he is small, you will be setting your child on the road toward becoming a secure and independent person.

On the other hand, you want to guide your child, to help him learn how to live in concert with other people. So you will eventually help him to space out his feedings and to adjust his schedule so that he can get along well as part of the family. You cannot, of course, expect a tiny infant to be "reasonable" with his demands. To him, being reasonable means that he can reasonably expect to be fed when he cries and reasonably expect that you will somehow divine his other wants.

HOW MODIFIED DEMAND FEEDING WORKS

How, then, does a modified demand feeding schedule work? You change a strict demand feeding schedule—when the baby is fed every time he whimpers—into a modified demand schedule by your decisions as the other half of the nursing couple. You recognize that there are times when your baby might accept the breast but that he might need some other kind of care even more. You take your cues from your baby, but you interpret these cues. You recognize the fact that caring for a baby means much more than just nursing him. You remember that it is important to protect your own health—both physical and emotional. And you take into account the needs of other family members besides the youngest.

In general, you will have confidence in your baby's ability to set his pace for nursing and in your ability to keep up with him. You will nurse the baby whenever he seems to want the breast. If, for example, your baby wakes up crying about two or three hours after a feeding, you will offer him your breast. If he does not wake up for four or five hours, you will not wake him to feed him (except for certain exceptions, discussed on page 99). Since you want to stimulate your breasts as much as possible and help your baby to sleep well between feedings, you will offer him both breasts at each nursing.

Remember that offering your breast to your baby does much more than allay his hunger. It offers him the warmth of your body, the rhythms of your breathing and heartbeat, the comfort of your arms, the feel of your skin on his face. In his early weeks, your baby will want the breast often—for all these benefits, as well as for the milk.

The average breastfed baby will probably want to nurse as often as every two to three hours for his first few weeks of life. This is so different from the "ideal" four-hour schedule that the demand-fed bottle baby tends to work out for himself that you may be afraid you are not providing enough milk for your baby. Don't worry; this is perfectly natural. Because the breastfed infant digests his food so much more quickly than his bottle-fed counterpart, he is ready to eat again sooner. He will sometimes sleep for four or five hours between feedings—and at other times want to be fed almost hourly for several feedings.

You will probably find that your breastfed baby averages between eight and ten feedings during a twenty-four hour period until he is about a month old, when he will be nursing every three to four hours or so, or an average of six to eight feedings in twenty-four hours. By three months of age, he will probably have cut back to between three and five feedings a day.

Some babies put themselves on a fairly regular schedule that everyone is happy with, and then suddenly for no apparent reason, they clamor for more food. This may be because your milk supply is temporarily diminished (you may be upset or tired) or because the baby is going through a spurt of rapid growth that makes him especially hungry. At times like this, be flexible. A couple of days of feeding your baby much more frequently than you have been doing should stoke up your little eater with the vast quantities of food he needs, provide him with the comfort of being nursed, and increase your milk supply.

Or the baby may not necessarily be hungry. He may have a little cold or not feel up to par for some other reason and want his nursing sessions more for their comfort than their calories. Isn't it wonderful to be able to soothe a baby so easily? At times like this, you'll be especially happy that you are a nursing mother.

If, however, your baby seems to want to be fed very frequently (more often than every two hours for a newborn or every three hours for a month-old baby) for more than a day or two, check with your pediatrician. Continuing to maintain such a demanding schedule for more than a brief time would be hard on you—and might not provide your baby with what he needs, either.

WAKING THE BABY

Sometimes, as we said, you'll want to modify your baby's demands for the breast. While you ordinarily wouldn't wake your baby but would wait to feed him until he "asks" for a nursing, there are some occasions when waking seems to be in order. If you have a baby who confuses night with day—who regularly sleeps for five or six hours at a stretch during the day and begs to be fed almost every hour once you go to sleep, you can try to change his inner "body clock." Try waking him at three-hour intervals during the day; he will eventually realize that daytime is nursing time and nighttime is for sleep. Or if you have a very docile infant who sleeps often and nurses obligingly on a "bottle-baby" schedule, but is not gaining as quickly as your doctor feels he should be, try waking him a little more frequently—say, an hour before he would ordinarily awake for a feeding. You might also want to wake your baby sometimes to help him regularize his schedule somewhat to fit in with the rest of the household. Say you have other children to feed, it is coming on toward dinnertime, and the youngest member of the family has been snoozing peacefully for more than three hours. It is all right to wake him gently and feed him, so that you can go ahead and make dinner for the rest of the family without worrying about having to stop in the middle to nurse the baby.

WHEN THE BABY CRIES

Other modifications of a demand feeding schedule would encourage the baby to go a little longer between feedings. Suppose he has had a nice long nursing, gone to sleep the picture of contentment—and then wakes up an hour later, crying. Is he hungry? Maybe, maybe not. Does he need something from you? Definitely. Babies cry for a reason. This is the only way they have to ask for something. You may not be able to tell immediately what it is your baby wants, but you can usually find out. Don't be afraid of spoiling your baby by going to him when he cries. An infant cannot be spoiled by frequent handling; in fact, the handling itself may be what he is crying for.

When your baby cries two or three hours after his last feeding, you know immediately what to do for him—put him to the breast. But suppose he cries right after a feeding? What should you do? If he wakes up early occasionally, offer him the breast, and don't worry about what time it is. But if he is regularly waking and crying oftener than every two hours, or if he cries a lot right after his feedings, you'll want to try other ways of comforting him besides giving him the breast. Otherwise, you're likely to develop sore nipples and you're bound to become tired and irritable from being "on call" all the time.

Here are a few suggestions for soothing a crying baby:
- Pick him up and hold him. Your baby may have a full and comfortable tummy and want nothing more than your tender touch. A baby probably misses the rhythms of his life in the womb, when he felt his mother's heartbeat and breathing all day long. Sometimes he may be filled with vast unnameable yearnings to be held close and cuddled. If you hold him or rock him at times like

this, you can often soothe him. Also, if you are nervous and upset, your baby may be responding to your moods; a little rocking and cuddling might help you to relax, too.

• Change his diaper; some babies are uncomfortable with wet or soiled diapers, even though most don't seem to mind.

• Burp him; maybe a bubble of air trapped in his stomach is making him uncomfortable.

• Change his position in the crib: to his back, his tummy or his side, or with his head where his feet had been.

• Wrap him snugly in a receiving blanket; some infants feel more secure when firmly swaddled.

• Give him a little boiled, unsweetened water in a bottle. A few sips of water may fill his stomach temporarily, satisfy his sucking urge and give him the comfort of being held. The water goes through his system quickly and does not interfere with his appetite for the next feeding.

• If you have changed, burped, cuddled, swaddled, and watered the baby, all these maneuvers have probably taken up close to an hour's time. If the baby still seems unhappy after all of this, put him to the breast. He may be comforted by a few minutes of nursing—or he may really be hungry, after all.

• If he is still restless, try a pacifier as a last resort. Pacifiers have their place in baby care; they are wonderful tools that provide extra sucking time for those babies who need it, but they should not be used to "plug up" a baby every time he opens his mouth. By doing that, you may be covering up some other needs he has.

If you do give your baby a pacifier, you may want to give him one that was orthodontically designed to simulate the nursing experience as closely as possible, the Nuk Sauger "exerciser." This pacifier comes in two sizes: one for an infant and one for an older baby. The way its shape was arrived at is interesting. A sculpted reconstruction of a mother's breast was formed out of semi-flexible material and then given to a nursing infant. The baby's sucking shaped the nipple and formed a model for the manufactured product, which closely resembles the shape and feel of the human nipple in the baby's mouth. You may be able to get the Nuk Sauger from your drugstore or through your dentist. Or you can order it directly from Rocky Mountain Dental Products Co., P.O. Box 1887, Denver, Colorado 80201.

• If you have tried everything and nothing works and your baby seems to be crying "all the time," call your doctor. He may suggest that you bring the baby around to see him. He'll check the baby over, reassure you as to his health and give you some suggestions for making life run more smoothly.

All this is not to say that by your loving mothering, you will be able to keep your baby from ever crying at all. This is an impossible dream. Frustration and discomfort are a part of life. While you can try to keep them at a minimum for your small child, part of his growing up involves learning to deal with problems in his own way. Don't spring into action at the first little whimper from the crib. Babies often fuss in their sleep, find a more comfortable position and in a few minutes go back to snoozing peacefully. Some babies seem to need to cry lustily for five or ten minutes before they can let go of the waking state. Unnecessary handling at times like these will not help your baby to solve his own problems when he can, but will merely disturb him.

Even on a modified demand schedule, your day is pretty much at your infant's beck and call, at least for the first few months. You will have some free time between feedings, but it is likely to be cut up into fairly uneven and irregular patterns. You won't be able to eat dinner at the same time every night or to make plans more than a few hours ahead of time. If you have always been a very well-organized person, you may find it so hard to get used to this more fluid way of doing things that you decide to help your baby establish a more regular schedule. On the other hand, you may discover a whole new way of life and decide not to go back to living "by the clock."

HOW LONG SHOULD EACH FEEDING BE?

Probably the average nursing session will last for some forty minutes, allowing for about ten minutes on each breast and twenty minutes of bubbling, diaper-changing and cuddling. There is no hard-and-fast rule, however. Once your nipples are used to the suckling and your milk is well established, you can nurse for as long as you and your baby both want to stay with each other. A baby who is actively nursing will milk each breast in about five or six minutes; the rest of the time he will get a trickle of milk for his efforts and enjoy the sucking time. You can tell if your baby is really sucking for milk, as opposed to sucking for fun. If he's actively nursing, you can see his temples move.

These feeding sessions can be your best form of relaxation, a chance to put up your feet and enjoy television or a good book. Or you might use this time to read to your toddler, who can sit nestled by one side while baby brother nurses at the other.

If you have a baby who never seems ready to end his nursing sessions, maybe he would welcome the gift of a pacifier (see page 101). It's no substitute for you, but can help him satisfy his sucking needs.

HOW DO YOU KNOW WHEN THE BABY IS GETTING ENOUGH MILK?

One of the biggest problems of nursing, in the minds of many women, is that they cannot tell how much milk their babies are drinking. In a way, this is actually one of its biggest advantages, too, since the nursing mother is not tempted to urge her baby to drink more milk than he wants. If you feed your baby on a flexible modified demand schedule, your supply of milk should keep up with his appetite. If you are well and rested, you are virtually assured of having plenty of milk for your baby. Particularly if you don't worry too much about your adequacy as a milk provider.

After you have been home a while, you may find that your breasts are no longer hard and full the way they were in the hospital. This does not mean that your milk supply has diminished. The glandular changes in the breasts and the increased blood circulation cause their initial fullness. Once milk production is fully established, the breasts become softer and remain soft—even while they are producing copious amounts of milk.

You can satisfy yourself about the adequacy of your baby's rations in several ways. If he seems contented, sleeps well and cries for feedings at fairly well-spaced intervals, you can be confident that he is getting enough to eat. But most of us don't have such perfect babies. All babies cry—and some cry after every feeding. How can you tell whether a baby who cries a lot is crying from hunger?

One way is by checking his weight gain. But be careful not to fall into a common trap. We live in a competitive society, where the biggest is often considered the best. It is often hard for the new mother to avoid comparing her baby's weight gain with that of the baby next door. Your breastfed baby, though, is almost certain to gain more slowly than a bottle-fed baby, and he may even gain more slowly than another breastfed infant. The fact is that rapid weight gain is no guarantee of health. In fact, doctors are now investigating the possibility that our methods of feeding babies over the past couple of generations have stimulated excessive weight gain that may lead to obesity and heart trouble in later life.

The average breastfed baby gains from four to six ounces a week in the first month and between six to eight ounces a week during the next three months. This gain is likely to vary considerably from week to week, ranging from an ounce or two in one week to a whopping seven or eight ounces the next. Since these weekly fluctuations are so great, it's best to wait for your regular checkups at the doctor's office to weigh the baby. If you buy your own scales, you will be tempted to weigh your baby much too frequently and then worry unnecessarily. If you're really anxious and your doctor's not too far away, you can probably take the baby in for an occasional weighing. And remember, just like adults, babies don't eat the same amount of food at every feeding or the same every day.

Meanwhile, you can judge whether your baby's taking in enough food by checking his diapers to see what comes out. If he has six or more wet diapers a day with pale yellow urine and regular bowel movements (either frequent small ones or less frequent large ones), he is getting enough to eat. (If he's drinking a lot of water, however, the diaper test is not a reliable indication.)

Other signs of a well-fed baby are bright eyes, an alert manner and good skin tone.

Note: Do not try to test for hunger by offering the baby a bottle after nursing. The typical infant has such a strong urge to suck that he will usually take some milk from a bottle even if he isn't hungry.

HOW TO BUILD UP YOUR MILK PRODUCTION

Suppose you and your doctor feel that your baby is not getting enough milk. What can you do about it? Before you think about using supplementary bottles, follow these suggestions and in a few days you will probably be giving more milk.

- **Nurse your baby more frequently.** This is the best way to make milk, since the breasts take their cues from your baby's needs. The more milk he takes, the more they will make, in this classic example of supply and demand.
- **Express milk manually after each feeding for a few days.** This is a way to "fool" the breasts and

stimulate them to make more milk.

• Check your schedule. Are you trying to do too much? Remember—you need plenty of rest, especially in the early weeks. You should be napping at least once a day and more often if you can manage it. If you have older children and nobody to take care of them for the couple of hours when you might nap, bring them into your room to play so that you can at least lie down. Strip your life to bare essentials, and for the time being expend a minimum of effort. Appeal to your husband, your mother or your next-door neighbor for help with such essentials as marketing, cooking simple meals and doing basic laundry. Most people like to help a new mother, so take advantage of this willingness while you can. You can always help them out later on. Restrict your guests to those few close friends who won't expect you to have a spotless house and a plate of fresh-baked cookies on the table.

• Check your diet. Are you eating enough of the right kinds of foods and drinking enough liquids?

• Take extra vitamin B complex. Many nursing mothers have found that one to three teaspoons a day of brewer's yeast is helpful in increasing milk supply.

• Stay far away from bottles of formula—unless you have a baby who is so small or who has had such problems already in his young life that your doctor (not your baby nurse or your mother-in-law) feels he absolutely needs a temporary supplement after breastfeedings.

• Ask your doctor whether he advises temporary use of artificial oxytocin in nasal spray or tablet form to give your let-down reflex a boost.

• Make a special effort to relax before a feeding. Try some of the following suggestions, which have helped other nursing mothers:

✔ *Take an occasional glass of beer or wine, especially before the early evening feeding, which is likely to be the lightest.*

✔ *Eat a healthful snack just before a feeding.*

✔ *Drink a glass of water, milk, or juice before or during feedings.*

✔ *Lie down for a few minutes before the feeding, and then continue to lie down while you nurse.*

✔ *Listen to music before and during feedings.*

✔ *Do some light reading while nursing.*

✔ *Nurse in a quiet room.*

✔ *Take a hot shower shortly before a feeding.*

✔ *Nurse in a comfortable rocker with arms.*

✔ *Take an aspirin about thirty minutes before a feeding if your nipples are tender. (See Chapter Nine for suggestions on healing sore nipples.)*

✔ *Stretch out and take twenty deep breaths before nursing.*

✔ *Telephone a reassuring friend, preferably a successful nursing mother.*

The most effective milk-producer of all is self-confidence. It is a shame that so many nursing mothers in our society have so little assurance of their ability to be good providers. It's particularly sad since lack of confidence itself sets up a vicious cycle that causes the milk to diminish. Just tell yourself that millions of other women nurse their babies and you can, too. The stories you hear of other women who "didn't have enough milk" can almost all be ascribed to lack of motivation, lack of encouragement, lack of information, or lack of confidence. If you don't lack any of these attributes, you can provide all the milk your baby needs.

IF YOU HAVE TOO MUCH MILK

Occasionally, a woman will have so much milk that it

will spurt clear across the room from the uncovered breast and flow too quickly into the baby's mouth to be easily swallowed. The baby will gulp noisily, gasp, choke, and sputter during the feeding—and then stop nursing after only a few minutes, only to burst into pathetically loud wails. A baby forced to drink too quickly from such an over-active breast will swallow air, have uncomfortable air bubbles, hiccup, spit up, and not be able to satisfy his sucking needs.

This is an easy situation to correct. All you have to do is express the first torrents of milk until it starts to come in a steady drip. Your baby will then be able to drink more comfortably. If you have this much milk, you may want to offer just one breast at a feeding. If your other breast becomes uncomfortably full, you can express the milk and save it either for relief bottles or for contribution to a local milk bank for babies who need more breast milk than their own mothers can supply. (See Chapter Nine for instructions on expressing and storing breast milk.)

NIGHT FEEDINGS

It is the middle of the night, and everyone, including the family dog, is sleeping peacefully. Everyone, that is, except your new baby, whose lusty bawling pierces your sleep and announces that he wants to eat. You drag yourself out of bed and wonder when that happy day will come when you can once again have an uninterrupted night's sleep. This is hard to say. The age at which a baby gives up his night feedings seems to be an individual characteristic that is not related to his size at birth, his weight gain afterwards, the amount of food he eats in a day, or whether this food comes from the breast, the bottle, or the jar. An occasional baby gives up the middle-of-the-night feeding as early as six weeks, a great many more give it up at about three months, and some seem to need it for yet a few months longer. In the early weeks, you need that night feeding as much as your baby does, so that your breasts will continue to be well

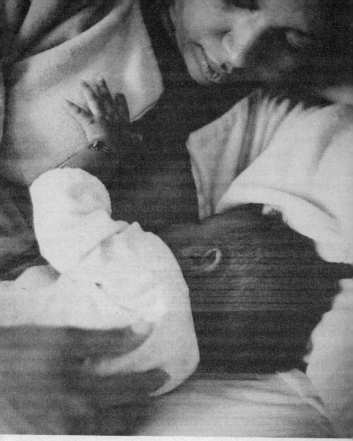

Nursing at night

stimulated and will not become engorged and uncomfortable by morning.

For the first month, when your baby is waking several times a night, you'll probably find it easiest to keep him in your room. That way, you can just reach over and bring him into bed with you. You don't have to bother changing him during the night unless he's absolutely drenched or seems uncomfortable. Just nurse him and put him back to bed. If you're afraid you might fall asleep while nursing, and your baby might get tangled in the bedcovers, make a point of sitting up.

By the time the baby is a month old, he will probably sleep better in his own room, where he can't hear you roll over in bed, and you can't hear all his little sleep sounds. Gradually he'll go longer between night feedings, until one morning you will spring out of bed, breasts full, to run over to his crib to see what is the matter. Nothing is wrong; your baby has just slept through the night for the first time.

If you don't mind terribly getting up at night, there's no age by which the baby *has* to sleep through, so you can just wait till he gives up the night feeding himself. But if the baby is a good size, say well over ten pounds, is eating often and well during the day, and if getting up with him makes you irritable, you may want to try to encourage him to sleep a longer stretch at night. Sometimes one of the following will work:

- Try giving the baby his late evening feeding a little later, maybe as late as midnight, in hopes that this will hold him until morning.
- Let the baby fuss for fifteen or twenty minutes when he wakes in the middle of the night; some babies quickly become resigned to waiting a while longer for mealtime, and go back to sleep.
- Let your husband go in to comfort the baby and offer him a few sips of water. From a very early age, your baby associates your looks and your smell with his feeding; if you go in to him at night, he will expect to eat. For this reason, his father may be more successful in getting him to go back to sleep.
- Try offering a pacifier. It may help your baby fall asleep.
- If you are really desperate, you may decide to grit your teeth and let the baby cry it out for a few nights. This is pretty drastic, but it seems to work well in some families.

DIAPER-CHANGING

Remember that the bowel movements of your baby are quite different from those of a bottle-fed baby. A grandmother or baby nurse used to bottle babies may look at your baby's stools, become worried about his health and consequently alarm you. So put their minds and your own at ease.

Your baby may move his bowels quite frequently, possibly after every feeding. Or he may move them only once a day, or once every three or four days. Or he might start out one way and change his patterns of elimination. His movements are likely to be quite soft, seedy and yellowish, like soft-scrambled eggs, with a little water around them. Sometimes there may be only a stain on the diaper. This is not diarrhea. The stools may come out easily, or the baby may seem to be straining quite a bit. This is not constipation. All these patterns are normal and healthy.

Sometimes the baby's stools may become looser in response to something you have eaten—large quantities of fruit juice, for example, or certain foods in the cabbage family. Try to discover the offending food and avoid it while you are nursing. Do not take any strong laxative at this time, because this can give your baby diarrhea.

When you are changing your baby daughter's diapers a few days after birth, you may notice some bleeding from the vagina. This is a false menstruation, due to hormones secreted by the placenta just before birth. This vaginal bleeding will go away in a day or two and is nothing to worry about.

YOUR SOCIAL LIFE

One of the nicest things about nursing a baby is that it excuses you from many obligations. For months, nobody will expect you to put in a full day's work, entertain for dinner, collect money for local charities, or be chairman of the PTA dance. In fact, when your baby gets a few months older and people assume you are "back in circulation," you'll find many occasions when you're glad you can say, "Oh, I couldn't do that—I'm nursing the baby, you know." This is a wonderful time in your life for pulling in your horns, forgetting outside pursuits, and enjoying being a homebody.

The time will come, though, when you want to go out and do things. Once the baby is three or four weeks old, there's no reason why you can't get out for an occasional visit with friends or a trip to a drive-in movie—and no reason you can't take the baby with you. When babies are this young, most of them are very agreeable to going out and being bedded down for the evening in carriage or car-bed. Should your nursling want to be fed, you are right there. The only danger in going out this way is that it seems so easy that you tend to over-do it! You start to go out so often and stay out so late that you tire yourself more than you realize. So be sensible.

If you feel easy about breastfeeding in front of other people, go right ahead. You need not feel apologetic or bashful about nurturing your baby the way mothers have done from time immemorial. Our society is indeed over-civilized when it makes women feel embarrassed to nurse their babies even in front of close friends and relatives, and causes many people to feel discomfiture at viewing this expression of maternal love. Fortunately, more and more women are shaking the bonds of false modesty that have in the recent past sent nursing mothers scurrying for absolute privacy. As more and more mothers feel more comfortable about nursing their babies when other people are around, their attitude will be contagious.

If you do feel shy about nursing in front of others, however, don't feel you have to force yourself to be "modern." When feeding time comes, just excuse yourself, go into another room and feed the baby. Most people will respect your wish for privacy. If you are in a public place where you simply cannot be alone, you can often find a quiet nook where you will be relatively unobserved. (If your husband is with you, he may be able to "read" a newspaper in such a way that it serves as a screen.) For ways in which you can plan your wardrobe for unobtrusive breastfeeding, see the section "Clothes for the Nursing Mother" on page 116.

By the time your milk supply is well established and your baby has developed a fairly regular schedule—sometime between four to eight weeks—you may want to go out occasionally without the baby. You may even miss one afternoon or evening feeding a week. Don't overdo this, since it's easy for your baby to develop a preference for the bottle, although one bottle a week should not have any ill effects on his nursing or your milk production. If you *are* going to offer an occasional bottle, be sure to start before the baby is two months old. Otherwise, he may absolutely refuse to take the unfamiliar rubber nipple. (Many a breastfed baby takes a bottle better from someone other than his mother, whose sweet smell he associates with her breast milk.)

If it is possible, express or hand-pump your milk when you are away. When you feel the tingling that signals the letting down of your milk, or at the time when you would ordinarily breastfeed, go into a powder room and express a little milk. You'll feel more comfortable, you'll be less likely to leak, and your breasts will get the regular stimulation that helps them to be good milk producers.

LEAVING A RELIEF BOTTLE

The simplest kind of bottle to leave is a prepared container of ready-to-feed formula that you can buy in the drug store, all sterilized, mixed, and ready to be given to the baby at room temperature. In order to provide your baby with a sucking experience similar to what he is used to, you may want to substitute the Nuk Sauger nipple, which resembles the human nipple more closely than does the standard nursing nipple.

By the time your baby is three months old, or weighs about thirteen or fourteen pounds, he can drink plain homogenized milk, cold from the refrigerator. Ever since large-scale studies of hospitalized premature babies showed that these babies did just as well or better by drinking ice-cold formula, mothers have been freed from the task of warming baby's bottle. The switch from your 98.6° breast milk to cold milk will not bother your baby. Just think of the various extremes of temperature that the normal diet contains.

Instead of formula or homogenized milk, you may prefer to leave your baby a bottle of your own breast milk, which you have previously expressed and refrigerated and frozen. You can express an ounce at a time after feedings, put it in a sterilized bottle, and keep it in the freezer till shortly before use. For detailed instructions on expressing and keeping milk, see Chapter Nine.

YOUR OLDER CHILDREN

If you have other children, you may wonder about their reactions to your nursing the new baby. You may be afraid that your feeding the baby in such an intimate way will make your other children especially jealous of him. Actually, your older children, particularly the one closest in age to the new one, will most likely show a certain amount of jealousy no matter how you feed the infant. This doesn't seem to be any worse when the baby is nursed.

You can expect your older ones to be on your lap or by your side as the baby is nursing. Accept this and make feeding times family times. One advantage of breastfeeding is that you will have a free arm to draw your toddler close to you, or to turn the pages of his favorite book. While the infant has your close touch and your breast, your older child can have your attention on his level. Show your other children in many ways throughout the day that they have not been displaced in your affections by the new baby, but do not let them feel that they have the right to deprive the infant of his right to be nursed at your breast.

Occasionally a toddler will ask whether he can nurse, too. Let him try. Chances are that he was just testing you; once

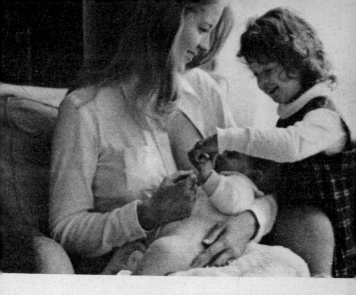

you give him your go-ahead, he won't do anything about it. He may laugh and forget about it, or he may even put his mouth to your breast for a minute but not know what to do once he is there. The suckling movements that come so naturally to a newborn seem to be easily forgotten, so that a baby who has nursed as recently as a month before may have already forgotten how to do it.

If you nursed your other children, you can emphasize to them that they were fed this way when they were infants, and now it is the new baby's turn. If you didn't breastfeed them, you probably won't volunteer this information. But if they are old enough and curious enough to ask you about it, you can be truthful. Explain to them that you didn't know much about breastfeeding when they were little—you didn't know that it was so good for the baby and so easy for you. But now that you do know more about it, you want to be as good a mother as you can to the new baby, just as you always try to do as much as you can for all your children. Most youngsters accept this simple explanation—and are, incidentally, happy to hear that even adults keep learning new things.

As a breastfeeding mother, you have a lovely opportunity to provide some elementary sex education in an easy, natural way. The child who sees his little brother or sister at the breast learns some of the biological differences between men and women, and gains a sense of the function and beauty of the human body. Your little daughter may be especially inspired by the thought that she will be able to care for her babies in this special way when she grows up.

Your older children can probably offer more help to you than you realize. Take advantage of their interest in being eager baby-entertainers, willing messengers who will fetch a clean diaper or toy or pacifier, and pleasant companions to you as they help you fold the laundry, set the table, or push the baby carriage. Isn't it nice to do the most routine everyday activities together as a family?

CLOTHES FOR THE NURSING MOTHER

You should have at least three nursing bras—one on you, one in the drawer, and one hanging up to dry. If you are leaking a great deal of milk, you will want to change bras or liners often, to keep your nipples from getting sore and your clothes from getting stained. To absorb leaking milk, put some type of lining inside your bra. Disposable nursing pads are sold in drug stores. These are comfortable and convenient, but if you don't want to go to the expense of buying them, you can easily make your own. You can fold your husband's old handkerchiefs and insert one in each cup of your bra. Or you can cut out four-inch circles from diapers or old tee shirts and stitch three or four thicknesses together.

A word here about leaking: This is usually common in the early weeks but stops being a problem within a couple of months. If you are still leaking through your clothes despite your precautions, try pressing your breast with the heel of your hand or your forearm when you feel the tingling that signals let-down.

While you are nursing, you will want to plan your wardrobe to make your life as easy as possible. This includes having as many clothes as you can that are washable and wrinkle-resistant and that don't need ironing. Try to choose prints or colors that won't give you away if a little milk leaks through. For the most part, separates—blouses or knit tops and skirts or slacks—are easier to manipulate than dresses. Skirts and pants with elasticized waists are especially good, since it usually takes a few months to regain your former waistline. (Ask your doctor whether you should be doing exercises to bring your figure back into shape.)

Button-front blouses are convenient, but so are knit pullovers, which can be easily pulled up to allow for modest nursing. When you're wearing a button-front blouse, you can nurse more modestly if you unbutton from the bottom up rather than from the top down. And when you wear a knit pullover, you'll find that the baby's body covers your bare midriff and the pullover covers the breast. Ponchos and loose-fitting cardigan sweaters are good aids to unobtrusive nursing.

If you sew, you can have a much more versatile wardrobe. And if you've never threaded a sewing machine in your life, this would be a good time to learn. You're home most of the time, anyway, and you can put your new skill to work making baby clothes, as well as nursing outfits. La Leche League newsletters give much ingenious advice on adapting dress patterns or altering dresses you already own. You can, for example, make horizontal seams clear across the bustline, or open up darts under it, and then insert invisible zippers. Or you can put zippers under the armholes of your sleeveless dresses. One ingenious nursing mother attached two fake pockets in strategic places with velcro. A flip of the mother's wrist lifted a corner of the pocket to make the breast accessible to the baby but protected from public view.

Finally, as a nursing mother, you should have one pretty scarf or shawl that you can drape decorously around your shoulders when friends drop in or the diaper man rings the bell in the middle of a feeding.

WHAT IS YOUR BABY LIKE?

All new babies have certain characteristics in common. They all have configurations of the face particularly suited for nursing: the receding chin and flat nose that allow them to get their faces in the right position at the breast, and the well-developed cheek muscles they need for suckling. They all sleep a lot, cry when they want something, eat often, and need the care of a mother or her substitute. They are all tiny, dependent, defenseless, and unutterably appealing.

However, we now know scientifically what mothers have always known: that each baby comes into this world a unique personality. Two psychiatrists and a pediatrician who conducted a long-term study of more than 200 children, found that individuals differ enormously right from birth in such characteristics as activity level, regularity, adaptability to change, acceptance of new situations, sensitivity to sensory stimulation, cheerfulness or crankiness, intensity of feelings, distractibility, and degree of persistence. From the time every person draws his first breath, he has his own distinctive temperament. Even while he was still in the womb, he had already begun to develop his own idiosyncrasies.

Since you will respond to your baby partly on the basis of his personality traits, it helps to recognize the type of temperament he has and to accept his uniqueness as an individual. You may recognize your baby immediately in the following profiles, or decide he is a combination of two or three, or realize that his personality is so unusual that we haven't even begun to describe him. Whichever way he is, the important thing is to accept him and love him for himself.

The Alarm Clock: These babies seem to have an inner clock that wakes them regularly, about every three hours. They sleep about the same time each day, tend to move their bowels the same time every day, and in general have predictable living patterns. They make life with baby easy.

The Bohemian: These are the babies who try mothers'

souls. They may sleep for two hours one morning, for fifteen minutes the next, and not at all the third. They can be ravenously hungry Monday morning and completely disinterested on Tuesday. They offer few clues to their wants. If left to set a self-demand schedule, they innocently run their mothers ragged. They can benefit from parental guidance in helping to regularize their living patterns.

The Good Eater: These babies come to the breast with a good appetite and an inborn knowledge of technique. They eat well, often sucking so vigorously that they develop blisters on the middle of their upper and lower lips. These don't bother the baby: the skin falls off, another blister forms and the cycle repeats itself till the baby's lips become hardened to his energetic nursing.

The Waiter: These babies don't become interested in nursing until about the fourth or fifth day. Sometimes this is because they have been sleepy due to childbirth medication; other times, they just don't feel like exerting themselves until the milk comes in.

The Dawdler: These are the slow eaters who may nurse a few minutes, then rest a while. Or they may mouth the nipple, taste the milk, and then set to work. Either way, they take the milk in their own good time and cannot be hurried.

The Dozer: These babies like to sleep, especially at mealtimes. Sometimes you can rouse a baby like this by dabbing him on the forehead with a sponge dampened with cool water. Or you can try expressing a little milk into his mouth. He'll swallow automatically and may resume active nursing. Sometimes playing with him before a feeding will encourage him to stay awake. If he usually falls asleep after nursing at the first breast, change his diaper at this time. He'll probably wake up enough to nurse for awhile on the other side.

The Over-Eager Beaver: These babies become so excited at feeding time that they move their heads quickly from side to side, grasp the breast, then lose it and end up screaming in frustration. You may have to make special efforts to calm down this kind of baby and put him back to the breast.

He gets the idea eventually.

The Biter: These babies come down hard on the breast, chewing it so forcefully that you can't believe they weren't born with a mouthful of teeth. You have to withdraw your nipples from his mouth when he starts this chewing. Remember to break the suction with your finger; don't pull your breast out of the baby's mouth. Otherwise, your nipples will become sore. Even an infant can learn not to bite the breast that feeds him. If your baby starts this while he is teething, withdraw the breast and say "No!" firmly every time he tries to bite. If you give a teething baby lots of toys specially designed to chew on, he'll be less likely to want to teethe on you.

The Spitter: These babies, usually fat and healthy, spit up milk regularly after practically every feeding. They may continue this until they are almost a year old and until you are convinced that you, the baby, and the house will always smell cheesy. (The smell is a lot milder while the baby is taking nothing but breast milk.) Sometimes it helps to prop a baby like this at a thirty degree angle for a while after his feeding, before you try to burp him. This helps the milk settle in the stomach, and discourages it from coming up with the air bubble.

The Lopsided Nurser: These babies develop a preference for one breast. The baby isn't lopsided, but the mother soon gets that way if she can't change her baby's mind. If one breast is producing more milk than the other, offer the less full one first at every feeding. The baby will drain this breast better and encourage it to produce more milk. When things are equalized, you can go back to alternating. Also, try to switch nursing positions: Hold the baby more vertically, or nurse lying down, or hold him with his head in front and his body toward your back, under your arm. If you can't influence your baby to give equal treatment, forget about it and wear a "falsie" on the smaller side when you go out. When you stop nursing, you'll regain your symmetry.

The Playboy (or *Playgirl*): Practically every baby falls

into this category at some time—usually about four or five months. By this time, he is more aware of the world around him and eager to show you how much he loves you. He will suddenly pull away in the middle of a feeding to flash you a bright, toothless smile. Or he will turn his head in response to a voice or a footstep. He will stroke your breast or your face with his little dimpled hand. He will play with the buttons on your blouse. This is such a beautiful way to cement a loving relationship that you should make every effort to relax and enjoy these longer, more playful feedings. If you occasionally want the nursing to go a little more quickly, try feeding the baby in a dark, quiet room free from distractions.

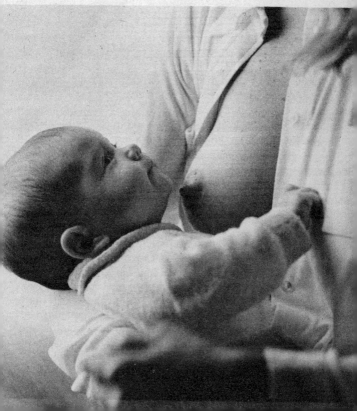

It takes about two months for you and your baby to become attuned to each other. The first few weeks, you are both busy learning how to nurse, and for the next few, you are perfecting the art. During this time you come to know what to expect of your life together. You learn that you have to nurse more often on those days when your baby is extra-hungry or your milk supply is extra-light. You learn that there are days when everything goes smoothly and days when nothing does. You learn that there are days when the baby is cranky and days when you are cranky. You know that you can cope with all these ups and downs because that is what life is like. By the time these first couple of months have passed, the trial and error period is over. You don't have long lists of questions about nursing. You know what to do—and you go about doing it. You and your baby are truly a nursing couple.

CHAPTER 7.

FOR FATHERS ONLY

Why, you may wonder, should we have a chapter for fathers in a book about breastfeeding? Aren't you pretty well left out of this part of your wife's life? That attitude, plus other feelings commonly shared by husbands of breastfeeding women, is what this chapter is all about.

Most new fathers are apt to feel a little bit shut out of the family circle, no matter how their babies are fed. Some men can accept these feelings more easily than others—but virtually *every* new father has them. You're not abnormal, you're not a monster, you're not a selfish brute, you're not immature for experiencing twinges of jealousy and hurt after the birth of your baby.

Remember, this is a difficult time for both you and your wife. Your familiar household routines are completely disrupted. You both have to learn how to accept your roles as parents. You have to take into account the needs and wants of a new person—a completely helpless and quite noisy addition to the family. In addition, you have added responsibilities toward your wife, who is recuperating from the physical demands of pregnancy and childbirth and coping with the hormonal changes accompanying these events. Both of you have mixed-up feelings, and each of you needs a lot of moral support from the other. And this is where you can be of immense help to your wife.

Your emotional support and encouragement are much more important to your breastfeeding wife than they would be if she had chosen artificial feeding. This is because she is likely to encounter disapproval, as well as disbelief, from her friends, her neighbors, her relatives, and maybe even her doctor. If *you* wholeheartedly support your wife in her desire to nurse your baby, she will be better able to handle the opposition from the rest of the world.

Your opinions on breastfeeding are important to your wife, and your encouragement is vital to her success in this womanly endeavor. Before you can encourage your wife to breastfeed your child, however, you yourself have to be convinced of the value of nursing for both mother and baby. You may have some worries about your wife's becoming a nursing mother—worries that may be allayed by information in these pages. You will probably be interested in reading Chapter One in this book, which discusses the benefits of nursing; Chapter Two, which answers some common concerns, such as the fear of a woman's losing her figure and her fear of being tied down; and Chapter Eight, which treats some of the ramifications of the relationship between man and wife.

You can learn a great deal by attending hospital-sponsored prenatal classes for expectant parents. If your wife is going to participate in prepared, or "natural", childbirth, and you want to be present during the birth, you will probably have to have some prenatal education before you can obtain permission to stay with your wife. Even if you are not going to be in the delivery room, you might still want to learn something about the childbirth process. The prenatal courses often discuss breastfeeding as well. Sometimes local chapters of such organizations as International Childbirth Education Association or La Leche League hold meetings for fathers, where you can air your questions and receive authoritative answers. Or you may want to take your questions to your family doctor, the obstetrician or pediatrician, or perhaps to a friend whose own wife successfully breastfed her children.

Breastfeeding definitely has its advantages for a father. You don't have to get up in the middle of the night and run for the bottle, a duty that many men feel they should shoulder. You don't have to worry about running out of formula at an inopportune time and having to dash around trying to find a store that's open. You can save money on baby-sitters, since it's very easy to take a nursing infant out with you—to friends' houses, drive-in movies, even on trips. When you do go places with a breastfed baby, there is less to lug—no bottles, cans of formula, sterilizing equipment, etc. Since the father is usually the one who carries all the paraphernalia required by a new baby, you'll appreciate this lightening of your load.

Most of all, you can revel in the fact that you have a truly feminine wife—a woman who may play tennis "like a man," perform superbly on a job, handle a screwdriver with ease when necessary, but still enjoy fulfilling herself as a woman. If you show your wife that you are proud of her femininity, you will help her to succeed at this womanly art.

You can support your wife most effectively if you are really convinced that breastfeeding is best for baby and mother. But even if you are not 100% convinced, you can appreciate the fact that *she* is and try to help her in all the ways you can think of. You can let her know that you are proud and happy to have a wife who so enjoys her own femaleness. You can let everyone else know that you stand behind your wife's decision. Speak to the obstetrician and the pediatrician to tell them that you support your wife's desire to nurse and that you will do anything you can to help her. Speak to those well-meaning friends and relatives who may be showing their disapproval of breastfeeding or doubting your wife's ability. Be her buffer and protect her against the subtle and the not-so-subtle disparaging remarks. If you make it plain that your wife is not to be discouraged from nursing, those near you will probably abide by your request and drop the subject.

One of the most important ways you can boost your wife's morale is to keep showing your interest in her as your wife. She is still your woman, not just the mother of your child. She needs to know that you still consider her interesting and attractive, that you still value her opinions as much as ever and that you still share interests besides the baby.

Do a lot of talking. Open communication between husband and wife is one of the most important elements of a good, solid marriage. You should both feel free to express your worries as well as your joys, your anger as well as your happiness. But, because of the great effect the emotions have on the course of breastfeeding, try to defer expressing your more negative feelings, at least for the first few weeks after your baby is born. Yes, you're angry because your wife forgot that phone call you asked her to make; yes, you're annoyed because she can't get along with your mother; yes, you're hurt because she sometimes seems distracted when you're talking to her.

A woman's ability to be a successful breastfeeder is closely related to her state of mind. The calmer and more relaxed she is, the better able she will be to produce and give milk. If your wife is tense after a quarrel, or if she senses your resentment toward her nursing the baby, she is bound to react physically as well as emotionally. The baby goes hungry, the mother gets frantic, and the father is caught in an emotional maelstrom. So, you see, you have an important role to play in the success of your infant's nursing. All this is not to say that you should stifle all your feelings—only that you try to deal with them in as adult a way as possible and to spare your wife, at least in her early weeks of nursing, as much emotional upset as possible. Later, when you confess to her how self-sacrificing you were, she'll appreciate you all the more!

Try to remember that your wife is probably busier and more wrapped up in her daily schedule with her first baby than she has ever been before and will ever be again, that the hectic pace of these first few weeks does recede, and that she will become more calm and less anxious about her new responsibilities.

If you can think to take some photographs of your wife nursing your baby right from the very beginning, you'll have something meaningful to look back on in later years. Also, you'll be telling your wife that you think she is beautiful when nursing your child.

There are many practical ways you can help your wife too. In our society, where so much masculine work does not involve hard physical labor, there is much less of a sharp distinction between work that is appropriate for a woman and that for a man. There is no longer any stigma attached to a man's shouldering some of the household duties, just as there is no stigma attached to a woman's mowing the lawn or taking out the garbage.

Every woman needs a great deal of rest after giving birth. Her body has to recover its strength, even while her sleep is constantly being disturbed. While a run-down nursing mother can produce milk, the effort will take its toll in her own health, and in the quality of care she can give to her baby and to the rest of her family. So see that your wife rests enough. If you can afford to hire someone to come in to help with the housework, your investment will pay off in your wife's good spirits, her quicker return to normality, and in a better cared-for house and family. If this is out of the question, pitch in yourself and do some of the marketing, the cooking, the vacuuming, the laundry. Bring home dinner occasionally —a pizza, a couple of cartons of Chinese food, or a basket of fried chicken. Ignore the dust balls under the coffee table.

One common worry among husbands of wives who plan to breastfeed is that there will be no way in which they can help to care for the baby. This fear, while very real to some men, has to bring a smile to the face of any experienced mother and father. There is so much more to taking care of a new infant besides feeding him! If you want to become close to your baby, you can do so much for him; you can be just as tender with him as any woman might be—with no loss to your masculinity. Just because your wife went through nine months of pregnancy, bore your child and is now nursing him, does not mean that she is the only parent who can care for him. For example, you can get the baby from his crib to take him in for his feedings. You can walk him or rock him when he is fussy. You can change his diapers—and you'll appreciate the fact that the completely breastfed baby's diapers smell much sweeter than do those of the artificially fed baby. You can baby-sit, giving your wife an afternoon or evening out. And when the baby is old enough to take an occasional relief bottle, who can give it to him better than his daddy?

At home with your family, and especially with your small children, you can let down that hard shell you wear all day at work. You can free yourself to express those warm, tender expressions of emotion that are yours to give. A man who can freely give and take loving feelings can know completion as a human being.

If you have older children, one of the nicest things you can do for them—and for your wife—is to lavish extra time and attention on them after your wife comes home with the baby. If *you* feel pushed to one side a little, imagine how *they* feel. Try to plan some outings with them and some special treats when they can have your undivided attention. The extra time you spend with your older children will mean a great deal to your wife, as well as to the children themselves, since her mind will be more at ease, knowing that they are happy while she is taking care of the completely dependent infant.

You may be thinking, "It's all very well for you to tell me to spend more time with my children, but I work all day and I'm tired when I come home. Besides, I have too many other things to do around the house—I just don't have the time." If your boss asked you to make a special effort, you would do it, wouldn't you? Now think—are your children really less important than your boss? You can create extra time by waking up fifteen minutes earlier or by setting aside a few minutes when you come home at night. If you consider this extra time with your children a necessity, you will be able to carve it from your busy day.

Far from feeling like that fifth wheel, you will find that in your important role of father, you are vital to the well-being of your family. What a wonderful feeling of pride you will have, knowing that you have made a major contribution to the life of your family.

CHAPTER 8.

SEX AND THE NURSING MOTHER

FEMALE SEXUALITY

In the realm of sexuality, the human male has but one string to his bow—his interest in and performance of sexual intercourse. It is largely around this one activity that male sexuality is defined. A man is generally considered a fulfilled sexual being if he is able to attain orgasmic satisfaction through intercourse.

The sexuality of the female of our species, however, is much more wide-ranging, involving the menstrual cycle, sexual intercourse, pregnancy, childbirth, and lactation.

All five of these phases are controlled to a large measure by the interaction of many of the hormones released inside a woman's body. Estrogen, progesterone, testosterone, FSH, LH, oxytocin, prolactin are among the hormones that direct a woman as a sexual being. Some of these substances manage the course of the menstrual cycle, causing ovulation and subsequently fertility. Some come into a dominant position during pregnancy. Others signal the onset of labor, the production and release of milk, and the climax of orgasm. Most of these hormones have more than one function. While some are more active during one phase of the female cycle than are others, the interaction among them is responsible for some remarkable similarities in the various sexual phases.

The most dramatic characteristic common to all five phases is the degree to which each one can be influenced by outside pressures and emotional reactions.

- The most regular *menstrual cycle* can be disrupted by excitement or anxiety. A bride, for example, may have carefully set the date for her marriage—and yet still menstruate on her wedding day. Or the tension of a job or family crisis may bring on or suspend a woman's period.
- The tremendous impact of outside influences on

sexual intercourse is obvious to any woman who just "can't get in the mood" for sex because of the distractions of financial, family, job, or health problems. Or a woman at the brink of orgasm may be "turned off" by a piercing yell from the nursery, the ringing of the telephone, or a fear that her privacy is about to be invaded.

• *Conception* itself is affected by emotional influences. Ovulation can be either stimulated or repressed by psychological factors. What else could account for the common phenomenon of the couple who try for years to have a baby, finally give up trying to conceive, adopt a child—and then find that the wife has finally become pregnant?

• Outside events also influence *childbirth.* An emotional or physical shock often brings on premature labor. And the very quality of labor and delivery—their ease and duration—has a direct relationship to the mother's anticipation of childbirth. The woman who is frightened of giving birth is apt to have a much more difficult delivery than the woman who understands the physiology of childbirth.

• Finally, mothers and midwives alike have long known that a woman's ability to give milk to her baby is influenced by such factors as pain, embarrassment, or emotional conflict. Recently, Drs. Michael and Niles Newton confirmed this observation in the laboratory, proving that a successfully nursing mother will give significantly less milk when she is distracted by annoyances and pain during feedings.

Many other phenomena are common to more than one phase of female sexuality.

• The breasts enlarge just before menstruation, during pregnancy, just before orgasm, and during lactation.

• The nipples become erect upon sexual stimulation, during childbirth, and during lactation.

- The uterus contracts during orgasm, childbirth, and lactation.
- Body temperature rises during ovulation, childbirth, orgasm, and lactation.
- A woman usually feels an urge to take care of her loved one in connection with a successful sexual relationship, during pregnancy, after childbirth, and during lactation.
- The hormone *oxytocin* surges through a woman's body during orgasm, during childbirth, and during lactation. It is this hormone that causes the uterus to contract and the nipples to become erect. Oxytocin is also the stimulus for the milk-ejection reflex, and nursing mothers commonly report that milk spurts from their breasts when they reach orgasm.

Female sexuality, then, involves a complex series of responses that carry over from a woman's reproductive capacity to her maternal functions. Yet in our society, woman's interest in sexual intercourse—in achieving her own orgasm and in helping her man to achieve his—has been stressed, while those elements of feminine sexuality related to childbirth and to lactation have been virtually ignored.

Childbirth and coitus resemble each other in many ways. Niles Newton, a psychologist and mother who has pioneered in the study of female sexuality, has recorded such similarities as the type of breathing, facial expressions, body position, abdominal and uterine muscle movements, clitoral engorgement, unusual body strength and flexibility, relief from inhibitions, and similar sensory perception and emotional reactions. Today's woman is exhorted to be more aware of her responses during lovemaking so that her enjoyment will be enhanced. Yet when this same woman is giving birth, she is likely to be sedated to such an extent that she will be largely unaware of her reactions. Women are rarely encouraged to enjoy childbirth, unless they belong to that small but growing body of individualists who seek out doctors and hospitals that encourage prepared childbirth, in which the mother is informed, awake, and participating.

Lactation also provides a woman with some of the same sensations as coitus: contractions of the uterus, erection of the nipples, and a rise in body temperature. Here again, the typical nursing mother is manipulated in such a way that she has to overcome great odds to sit back and enjoy breastfeeding. She is separated from her baby immediately after birth, kept from him for a period of time that may last as long as twenty-four hours, permitted to feed him only when it is convenient for hospital personnel. What would happen to marital relationships if we prescribed the same type of restrictions on sexual intercourse as we do on lactation? Sexual disaster, most likely.

We are currently experiencing an educational revolution involving the sexual relationships between men and women. We are learning more about the actual physiological mechanism of the acts of sex. We are overturning prudish taboos that have prevented men and women from experiencing the heights of sexual fulfillment. We are encouraging free communication between husband and wife about their sexual relationship. We are gaining an attitude of acceptance toward any manifestation of physical love between man and wife that is not distressing to either partner. Many married couples are finding that their sexual rapport is flourishing in such an open climate. Now we have to be just as open and understanding about those aspects of sexuality in the maternal role.

THE SENSUOUS NATURE OF BREASTFEEDING

In their landmark study, *Human Sexual Response,* Dr. William H. Masters and Mrs. Virginia E. Johnson included the results of interviews with 111 women who participated in the clinical research program while they were pregnant. These women talked about their sexual behavior, feelings, and responses during pregnancy and immediately following childbirth. Of this group, only twenty-four women breastfed their babies, even though Masters and Johnson were apparently encouraging in their attitudes toward nursing.

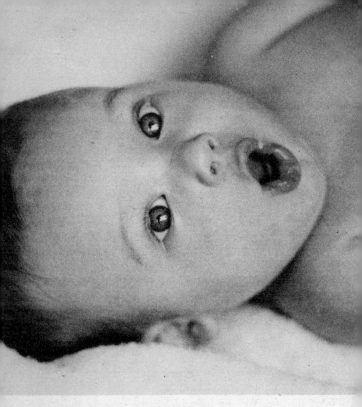

Some of these nursing mothers reported experiencing sexual arousal while suckling their babies. Three incidents of orgasm experienced while nursing were included in the Masters and Johnson reports. While such orgasm does occasionally occur, it seems to be quite rare among nursing women in the general population. (Unless it is more widespread than we think, but is not generally acknowledged.) Some form of sexual gratification, however, is commonly recognized. Some women experience clitoral sensations during nursing, with accompanying vaginal lubrication.

Most often the sexual satisfaction of nursing seems to take the form of a calm feeling of completion. Instead of the intensity and excitement of orgasm, the successful nursing mother experiences a sense of satisfaction similar to the euphoria that follows orgasm. She feels a happy combination of physical and emotional fulfillment.

It should not be surprising that breastfeeding has its sensual components. For many women, the breasts are highly erogenous zones, sensitive to the slightest touch and capable of sending messages of excitation throughout the body. Some women even reach orgasm from having their breasts fondled. During lactation, of course, the breasts are constantly stimulated both by the mother's own handling and by the baby's extensive sucking and sometimes frequent stroking.

In addition, rhythmic movement is known to be sexually stimulating to some women. Women have been aroused by riding in a car or on horseback and even from operating foot treadle sewing machines! The common use of a rocking chair by the nursing mother may enhance her sensual pleasure while it lulls and comforts her baby.

Unfortunately, those women who do experience sexual arousal during nursing are apt to feel guilty—so guilty that they may wean their babies early and refuse to nurse future children. In our society sexual feelings are supposed to stay in their place—to come out of hiding only when a culturally determined suitable partner is present. Yet we are sexual beings, and our sexual feelings spin a thread that runs through the fabric of our entire lives. It is truly a shame that more women who realize sexual stimulation from breastfeeding cannot relax and enjoy these pleasurable sensations.

Of course, many women do appreciate the sensuous nature of breastfeeding. They realize that nursing is supposed to be enjoyable for both mother and baby. If it were not, our species could never have survived the thousands of years when no substitute for human milk was available. Indeed, the good feelings associated with breastfeeding may just be a canny wile employed by Mother Nature to strengthen the bond between mother and baby in the early months of life.

Many women find no measure of sexual gratification in breastfeeding. They have no sexual feelings to repress or to feel guilty about, since they enjoy nursing their babies but in a purely asexual way. In his book, *Sexual Behavior in the*

Human Female, Dr. Alfred C. Kinsey stated that only half of all women seem to derive any satisfaction from having their breasts handled—and that both oral and manual stimulation of the female breasts is often more exciting to the man who touches than to the woman who is touched. A woman whose breasts are not normally erogenous is not likely to become erotically stimulated by the sucking of her infant. And even a woman whose breasts ordinarily respond to her husband's touch or kiss may find that during lactation, they become almost insensitive to touch—his as well as his baby's.

There is no right way or wrong way for your body to respond sexually to the nursing experience. You can be a successful nursing mother if you do become erotically aroused by breastfeeding—or if such feelings are the farthest thing from your mind.

THE SEX LIFE OF THE NURSING MOTHER

According to the Masters and Johnson findings, nursing mothers are more eager to resume sexual relations after childbirth than are women who do not breastfeed. As a group, the twenty-four mothers in the Masters and Johnson study who were breastfeeding their babies three months after childbirth had become more intensely interested in resuming sexual relations with their husbands and had wanted to do so sooner than did the non-nursing mothers. In fact, the nursing mothers generally reported that they had even more erotic feelings now than they had had before they became pregnant. Most of these women wanted to resume sexual activity within two to three weeks after childbirth.

And during the course of a study on the importance of information and support in the success of breastfeeding, psychologist Dr. Alice K. Ladas asked more than 1,000 nursing mothers several questions relating to their sexual relationships. While Dr. Ladas herself warns that her findings must be viewed with caution since they are based on self-reports about a highly emotionally-charged subject, it is still noteworthy that 30% of the mothers reported that their sexual relationships with their husbands had improved after nursing, while only 2.5% reported worsened relationships. Most of the women who said they now had a better sex life had considered their sexual relationship excellent before nursing, while all the women in the other category said they had had a poor sexual adjustment to begin with.

One mother commented, "There is something very earthy about nursing a child that can pleasantly affect the husband-wife relationship. And I also feel that a good breastfeeding experience makes you more open and womanly." Another said, "Because of nursing, I felt there ought to be a better feeling between husband and wife . . . and with a bit of help, it didn't take long. I was able to have orgasm which I had never had before."

Nursing mothers, however, seem to fall into two distinct camps. Some are like the group in the Masters and Johnson study. During lactation, these women experience increased sexual appetites and enjoy a much less sexually inhibited relationship with their husbands. Other women find that they are not nearly as interested in sex for the first six months after childbirth as they had been before or will be again.

A member of the first group—those women who are sexier while nursing—might be particularly sensuous and more comfortable with her own body than the average woman. She may have fewer feelings of embarrassment about handling or exposing her breasts. She may even welcome the opportunity to breastfeed as a chance to experience a new kind of bodily sensation. She may have especially erogenous breasts that respond erotically to the constant stimulation of the baby's suckling. Or the woman who is aroused sexually during lactation may have unusually high stores of oxytocin in her system. While this potent chemical is contributing to her success as a nursing mother, it may also produce increased levels of eroticism. One mother has said, "Of course, I didn't always feel sexy when I was nursing the baby—which is a good thing while I was feeding her eight to ten times a day!—

but sometimes the combination of nursing her and seeing my husband in bed next to me made me want to rush through the feeding so that Bob and I could make love."

In her book *Nursing Your Baby*, Karen Pryor, a biologist and a mother who nursed her own three children, described the women in the second group as being "compliant about sexual relations without actually being eager." Mrs. Pryor says that this may be due to the fact that "nursing a baby provides some of the fringe benefits of sex: closeness to another person, a feeling of being admired and cherished, and the reassurance that one is needed and wanted."

Many new mothers are less interested in sex for a while—whether they nurse or not—just because they are too tired to think about it. Taking care of a baby is hard work. Furthermore, the new mother must adjust to the constant interruption of her night's sleep. Add to this a first-time mother's concern about her ability to care for her new baby, and it is easy to understand some women's temporarily diminished interest in lovemaking.

A physiological reason for such reduced interest may be the not uncommon loss of sensitivity from nipples and breast surface during lactation. Some women also find that their nipples lose their ability to become erect on stimulation, even though they still become elongated in the baby's mouth. This apparent lack of erectility may be a true physiological reaction, or it may be nothing more than an optical illusion. Sexual arousal brings about an increase in the size of a woman's breasts and as the areolae swell during this breast expansion, it seems that the nipples, which have become erect in the first stage of sexual excitement, now lose their erection. Laboratory investigation has found, however, that the nipples only look shorter because they are partially masked by the swollen areolae. Since the breasts also grow larger during lactation, the same process may be taking place, with the enlarged areolae partially masking the erection of the nipples. (The already expanded breasts of the nursing mother do not increase further upon sexual excitation.)

In any case, whether you are "compliant about" or eager to resume sexual relations with your husband, you probably have many questions about lovemaking. You wonder how soon you should go back to enjoying regular sexual relations —and whether you should restrict your activities in any way, for your own sake or for your baby's.

Your doctor will most likely advise you not to engage in sexual intercourse until after your post-partum examination. While most obstetricians schedule this examination for six weeks after delivery, some physicians feel that they can assess a woman's recovery from childbirth as early as three weeks after the baby's birth. Ask your doctor to explain to both you *and* your husband the reasons for this abstinence. If your husband understands the reasons behind a temporary ban on intercourse, he will be much more amiable about observing it. (He will also be less likely to suspect that you made up the whole thing because you are more interested in the baby than in him.)

If both you and your husband feel free to maintain your sexual relationship—even without intercourse—you will be able to affirm a continuity in this very important area of your marriage. Even during times in your life when sexual intercourse may not be medically appropriate, you can still show your physical love for each other by "making love." You can, for example, still enjoy the sex play that you ordinarily engage in before coitus. And you and your husband can satisfy each other sexually through oral or manual alternatives to sexual intercourse. Even just tender, affectionate fondling of each other's bodies will help to preserve the intimacy of your relationship through this important time in both your lives.

Briefly, the reasons why you would want to postpone intercourse after childbirth relate to the need for the vaginal canal to re-develop the micro-organisms that protect it from infection; for the episiotomy (the incision commonly made during childbirth to expand the vaginal opening) to heal; for the uterus to return to its former size; and for the general tenderness in the perineal area to disappear. (Even after your doctor gives you the go-ahead, you may find that this tenderness causes some discomfort the first few times you engage in sexual intercourse; this is normal and only temporary.)

As you can see, then, the reasons for delaying intercourse after childbirth have to do with the vaginal region alone—and not with the fact that you are breastfeeding. Breastfeeding itself need not interfere with your love life in any way. One young woman who was nursing her three-month-old baby confided to a friend that she was reluctantly going to switch the baby to the bottle, because she was concerned about her marital relationship. Her husband had observed his vows of chastity long enough, he said, and by this time he had offered her her choice of "the baby or me." Situations like this probably account for many cases of early weaning, when in actuality they need not. There need not be a choice: You can be your husband's sexual partner during the time you are nursing your baby, and you can share your breasts with both baby and husband. Your breasts do not have to stop performing their erotic function just because they are now performing their biological function.

There is no reason why your husband cannot stimulate your breasts both manually and orally during the length of time you are nursing, if this is enjoyable to you both. In fact, Dr. Robert A. Bradley, a Denver obstetrician, recommends oral and manual manipulation by the husband of his wife's breasts during both pregnancy and lactation, since he feels that frequent handling of the breasts helps to prevent sore nipples. So you can relax and enjoy yourself as you follow doctor's orders.

Your husband won't be stealing candy from his baby if he gets an occasional swallow of your good milk. There is plenty more where that came from, and as you remember from the discussion in Chapter Five, the more milk that is removed from the breasts, the more will be produced. (We heard of one mother who went away for the weekend with her husband but without her baby—and the baby's father performed the toothsome duty of maintaining his wife's milk supply!)

You may find, particularly in the first couple of months, that your breasts become quite hard and tender an hour or two after a feeding. At these times, intercourse in the positions you may have been used to might be uncomfortable for you. So use your ingenuity. This might be the perfect time to experiment with those other lovemaking positions that you had always wondered about but never tried. You might even discover something you like better than your former "tried and true." In any case, the tenderness of the newly lactating breast goes away soon. After a couple of months, it will not be a factor in how you do what you do.

A frequent and dramatic sign of orgasm in the lactating woman is the spurting of milk from both breasts during and immediately after orgasm. Usually, the milk flows more slowly from the breast that has been suckled more recently. While some nursing women who experience this ejection of milk during orgasm keep their bras on to avoid leaking some milk, many another feels that a few spots on the sheet are a small price to pay for sharing with her husband the proof of his ability as a lover.

CONTRACEPTION

For years, lactation has been recognized as a deterrent to pregnancy but not a guarantee against it. When you see your obstetrician for your post-partum examination, you should discuss with him the means of contraception you will use when you are nursing, if you do not want to conceive again right away.

You will definitely not want to take oral contraceptives for reasons explained in Chapter Four.

Some alternate methods of birth control are the IUDs, or intrauterine devices (98% effective)*; cervical caps or

---

* These measures of relative effectiveness were reported by Drs. Roberts Rugh and Landrum B. Shettles in their book, *From Conception to Birth,* published 1971 by Harper & Row Publishers, Inc., New York City.

diaphragms (86–88% effective when used with spermicidal jelly); condoms (83–88% effective); or the use of vaginal suppositories, jellies or creams (about 80% effective). The rhythm method (74% effective) cannot, of course, be relied upon until your menses return on a fairly regular basis. The only contraceptive method that is 100% effective is, of course, abstinence. Taboos on sexual intercourse with a nursing mother have been observed in many different societies, probably as a means of spacing children. Now, however, a choice of several dependable and safe methods of contraception allow the lactating woman to enjoy being a wife as well as a mother.

YOUR HUSBAND IS STILL YOUR LOVER

The months following the birth of the first child constitute a difficult period of time in a marriage. Like any other new experience, you are likely to welcome the advent of parenthood with mixed emotions. The birth of your first baby brings home to you and your husband more dramatically than any other event in your lives the recognition that you are no longer children but adults, now responsible for another human being. Eager as you may be to grow into this phase of life, you may be anxious about what it will mean and what will be expected of you. If you and your husband have developed open communication before the arrival of the baby, you will have a good base to help you make your adjustments to parenthood. And there are many adjustments to be made.

Like every other woman in the world, you have to learn to be a mother. It does not happen magically via labor and delivery. You need time and practice to feel at home in your new role. Meanwhile, you are likely to worry about your ability to be a good mother. Your husband has his own conflicts to struggle with as he faces up to the responsibility of fatherhood. Yet all too often, both husband and wife will assume that their partners know how they feel, and neither one openly expresses his real concerns.

For example, you may suddenly find, as you struggle in the

morass of diapers and colic and nursing schedules that you would like to be a little girl again and have someone else care for you and your baby. But you're a mother now—how can you admit this? Meanwhile, your husband, who is awed by the competent way you feed, bathe, and diaper the baby, sees only your outer shell of self-assurance. You may seem so capable in carrying out your maternal responsibilities, and as a nursing mother so self-sufficient, that he underestimates your need for him. At the same time, he needs your assurances that he has not slipped to second place in your life. While he recognizes intellectually that the baby requires a great deal of your time and energy, he may not be able to help resenting all the attention lavished on the newborn—attention that was formerly his alone. In addition, he sees you sharing with the baby not only your time, energy, and attention, but also the breasts that were formerly revealed only to him. Is it any wonder that he should be a little jealous of his own baby?

Such feelings are natural, but many husbands are ashamed of feeling this way and will not admit them. Others express them quite openly. Aware that your husband may feel this way, you can show him that he is still the most important man in your life and that your love for him has not diminished because of your love for his baby. There are many ways you can do this. The most important thing is to recognize the need for extra effort on your part at this time to preserve the relationship that you had before the baby was born and to adjust to the demands and joys of motherhood without forgetting that you are still a wife.

The following suggestions might help you both over some rough spots:

- *Disruptions of the dinner hour seem to hit some husbands harder than anything else. You can minimize these by waiting until right after you have fed the baby to put the finishing touches on your dinner. Plan meals that take a minimum amount of evening preparation, such as casseroles that can be readied early in the day, simple meats that can be broiled in* minutes, and stews that won't mind waiting. These are all ideal during the first three months, when the baby's schedule is apt to be irregular. This is a good time to treat yourselves to Chinese food, pizza or fried chicken that can be delivered to your door.

- You can make the simplest meal a romantic one by lighting a couple of candles and opening a bottle of wine—even though you know you're squeezing this tête-a-tête in between feedings of the baby.

- If you're used to having a drink before dinner with your husband, don't give it up. Since the nursing mother has a free hand, it's easy to feed the baby right through cocktail time. This will provide a quiet interlude for both you and your husband—and may even help your milk to flow more freely.

- Plan at-home evenings, when the phone is off the hook and you are not "at home" for company. They may provide the relaxed time together that you and your husband need.

- Just because you're nursing, don't feel that you can't leave the baby at all. Plan an evening out once a week, so that you and your husband can have a "date" and enjoy each other's company in a carefree way. Leave the baby with a competent sitter—possibly a student nurse from your local hospital, an older woman or a college student. Leave a relief bottle filled with either your own milk that you have hand-expressed earlier in the day or with prepared formula. Once your milk supply is well established (usually by the end of the first month), it won't hurt to miss one feeding, and it will be good for the baby to get used to being cared for occasionally by someone else.

- Watch your appearance. You always look great to the baby, but when your husband comes home at night, he'll appreciate seeing you with your hair neatly combed and your clothes fresh and free from spit-up milk.

- *If nursing has given you the best-looking figure of your life, make the most of it. Wear something seductive occasionally. Wear clothes that show off your new measurements. You may have them only while you're nursing, so capitalize on them while you can.*

- *If you're eager to resume sexual relations with your husband, don't be shy about letting him know. He may be waiting for a signal from you. If you couldn't care less, try to work up some enthusiasm. You'll be glad you did.*

- *Bring your husband into the family circle. If he's interested in doing things for the baby, don't limit him to fetching and carrying but encourage him to hold the baby, to play with him, even to bathe him. If, like many men, your husband is not terribly interested in doing things for the young infant, don't push him. His attitude will probably change the first time his baby smiles at him.*

As a nursing mother, you are a lucky woman. You have both husband and child to love—and the opportunity to give of yourself to each of them. You have fulfilled your birthright—that cycle of sexuality that only a woman can know.

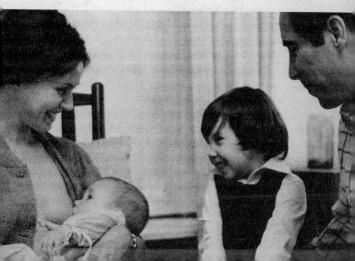

CHAPTER 9.

POSSIBLE PROBLEMS AND SPECIAL SITUATIONS

Because we want this book to be as helpful as possible to as many mothers as possible, we are including much material in this chapter that you probably won't need. But if you *should* run into any of these situations, you will want to know what to do. If you have a special problem, look it up in the index. But remember—because every mother and every baby is an individual, it is impossible for any book to cover every single contingency that might arise; and it is just as impossible to prescribe one solution that will apply to every nursing couple. If you have a special question, call your doctor. Or, when something troubles you, it can be wonderfully reassuring to talk to a successful nursing mother who may have dealt with the very problem you are now facing. If you don't know such a woman, ask your pediatrician whether he knows someone you might contact. Or call a La Leche League representative, who may know other nursing mothers in your area.

If you encountered a nursing problem with your last baby, don't assume that it will occur again. Breastfeeding history does not necessarily repeat itself. Each nursing situation is unique, and you will most likely have smooth sailing this time.

As we said, you should ask your doctor about many of the problems we'll be talking about in this chapter. If you have both an obstetrician and a pediatrician, you may wonder sometimes which one to go to. One physician has said, "The breast belongs to the pediatrician—unless it develops problems, when it becomes the property of the obstetrician." More simply, if the problem affects *your* health, call your obstetrician; if you're concerned about the baby, call your pediatrician. Or if one of your specialists is more interested in and knowledgeable about breastfeeding than the other, you'll probably want to call him first, no matter what the problem may be.

DISAGREEMENT WITH YOUR DOCTOR

Suppose your physician gives you some advice that contradicts the pro-breastfeeding information you have had. Or suppose he suggests that you stop breastfeeding the minute you run into a little problem. What should you do?

You have several choices. You can follow the doctor's advice and feel resentful; you can completely ignore the advice and feel anxious; you can switch doctors, even though you feel your doctor is capable in every other respect. None of these choices, of course, is really satisfactory.

Perhaps the best course to follow would be to ask the doctor why he is prescribing a certain procedure. For example, is he advising supplementary bottles after breastfeeding because he thinks it's generally a good idea to give them, or because he's afraid your baby is starving? Or, is he telling you to give solid foods at four weeks because this is his routine advice to mothers, or because he thinks your baby particularly needs them?

If your baby is sick or not thriving, or has some other special problem, it is very dangerous to blithely disregard your doctor's advice. If you find that you do not have confidence in what he tells you, you should, for your baby's sake, choose another pediatrician.

But if your baby is healthy, and you have reasonable confidence in your own theories, you may wish to openly discuss your differences with your doctor. One mother approaches such situations this way: "I have found a very effective way of talking to the doctor is to use the words 'I feel.' If you 'think' or 'insist,' he won't like it. But if you 'feel' you would like to do or not do something, this is a very gentle way to open the discussion, because nobody is going to step on your feelings." Another mother who ran into a disagreement with her doctor over when to start feeding solid foods took him some professional literature and said, "I'm terribly confused, doctor, because my husband feels one way and I feel the other. Won't you please help us out and read this?" (You can obtain professional literature from La Leche League, the International Childbirth Education Association, or your local medical library.)

SORE NIPPLES

Many women, especially fair-skinned blondes or redheads, experience temporary soreness the first few days after giving birth. If it is not severe and if it is relieved when the milk comes in and lets down for the baby, nothing special need be done. But if the nipples look red and chapped, or the pain during or after nursing is really bothersome, do something right away. Don't wait till the pain becomes unbearable. Soreness may set in on the second or third day of nursing or it may not appear until the second or third week. Or it may not show up at all. While most women experience some discomfort during early nursing, not all do. If you have prepared your nipples for nursing according to the suggestions in Chapter Four, you have a good chance of not running into this problem at all. But even if you do develop sore nipples, you needn't despair. You can heal them quickly and go on to be a happy breastfeeder.

To treat sore nipples, follow these suggestions:

- *Avoid all irritating substances. Do not use soap, alcohol, tincture of benzoin, witch hazel, or vaseline on your nipples.*
- *Use only mild creams such as pure lanolin, Vitamin A & D ointment or Massé cream.*
- *Keep your nipples dry. Snip out the plastic linings of your bra, which tend to trap the moisture. Change absorbent bra linings often. Walk around the house with your nipples*

uncovered as much as possible. Get small tea strainers from the five and dime, remove the handles and insert them in your bra to let air circulate around your nipples while you are dressed.

• *Expose your nipples to sunlight or a sunlamp. Be* very *careful, being sure to follow the directions given in Chapter Four.*

• *Take an aspirin, or a glass of beer or wine about 20 minutes before feeding.*

• *Use manual expression at the beginning of a feeding to start the milk flowing, so your baby won't be sucking vigorously at the breast before the milk lets down.*

• *Be sure the baby is taking the entire areola into his mouth, not the nipple alone. Do not let him chew on the nipple.*

• *Nurse your baby just as frequently but for shorter periods of time. Your breasts are less likely to overfill and your baby more likely to nurse gently.*

• *Limit sucking time to five minutes on the sore side (or on each side, if both nipples are sore). Give the baby a pacifier if he seems to need more sucking time.*

• *Offer the less sore breast first. This will give the milk a chance to let down in time for the sore side, and the baby won't be sucking as hard by the time he gets around to his second course.*

• *Change your position at each feeding. Lie down, sit up, hold the baby in different positions so that the pressure on different parts of the beast will be equalized.*

• *If a scab forms on the nipple during early nursing, leave it alone.*

• *Ask your doctor whether he thinks the administration of oxytocin might speed your let-down reflex.*

• *Occasionally sore nipples are caused by thrush, a fungus infection in the baby's mouth. If your baby has the milky white spots inside his mouth that are symptomatic of thrush, call your pediatrician. He will tell you what to do to clear up the baby's mouth and may also have suggestions for treating your nipples. One method that often works is to wash the nipples after every nursing in a solution of one teaspoon of bicarbonate of soda to a glass of sterile water. Dry the nipples and apply a mild cream. Continue to nurse.*

• *A few mothers have reported to us that they have successfully treated sore nipples by taking vitamin C for a couple of days, two to three grams a day in 100 mg doses.*

Usually, by using a combination of some of the above methods, you will clear up the soreness in a few days and you won't have any more trouble. In rare cases, however, the condition may continue to worsen until the nipple cracks and bleeds and is absolutely too painful to permit the baby to suck. If this should happen, take the baby off the affected nipple for twenty-four to forty-eight hours and feed him by bottle. Express your milk by hand (without touching the nipples) or electric pump every three hours, or every time you would ordinarily be nursing the baby. Gradually resume nursing with short (five-minute) feedings on the sore breast, starting twice a day. Continue to express milk at other feeding times until the breast is well enough to work up to the full nursing schedule.

The use of a nipple shield is sometimes helpful for cracked nipples. The shield consists of a plastic cone attached to a rubber nipple. It fits over the breast, and the baby sucks from the rubber nipple, drawing milk from the breast by suction; the baby's mouth does not come into contact with the breast itself. Be sure to fill the shield halfway with sweetened water to avoid the discomfort to your breast that would otherwise be caused by the baby's sucking.

The benefits of the shield are limited, however. Even though the mother's nipple is protected somewhat, it does not get as much stimulation as it should for the production of adequate amounts of milk. As a temporary measure, though, the nipple shield is sometimes just enough of an aid to help a mother over a rough time.

ENGORGEMENT (SWOLLEN BREASTS)

This painful swelling of the breasts experienced by some women three to five days after childbirth is caused by a combination of the swelling of the tissues, the increased circulation of blood in the breasts, and the pressure of the newly produced milk. The breasts feel hard, tender, and tight. Engorgement can usually be prevented by feeding the baby on demand from birth and withholding formula and sugar water from him. If the baby nurses vigorously and frequently from the start, the chance of engorgement is greatly reduced.

If you do become engorged, the following procedures are helpful:

- Take an aspirin or other pain-reliever as your doctor directs.
- Wear a firm bra for support. But be sure it's not too tight. This can aggravate your discomfort and cause other problems.
- Apply ice packs to ease the pain and improve circulation.
- Apply heat by a heating pad, a small hot water bottle wrapped in a towel, or a towel soaked in hot water. Or take a warm shower. (This seems to contradict the previous measure, but both extremes of temperature seem to help this condition. Some women find relief in one or the other; some, alternate hot and cold treatments.)
- Ask your doctor whether he wants to prescribe stilbestrol (which temporarily inhibits milk production somewhat) or oxytocin (which helps the milk let down through the ducts).
- Express milk manually or pump a little bit before a feeding, to soften the breasts.

CLOGGED DUCT ("CAKED" BREASTS)

In this condition, which can occur any time during nursing, one or more of the milk ducts are blocked, and the milk cannot pass through them. You are likely to find a small lump on the breast which is reddened and painful to the touch. If not treated, infection can follow this condition. To treat it, do the following:

- Be sure your bra is not so tight that it is pressing on the ducts.
- Breastfeed oftener and longer, so the baby can help you empty the breast.
- Change position with every feeding, so the pressure of his nursing will hit different places on the breast, exerting pressure on different ducts.
- Hand-express milk from the affected breast after each feeding, to get out as much milk as possible.
- If dried secretions are covering the nipple openings, wash them off very gently after each nursing with a piece of cotton saturated with sterile water.
- Offer the sore breast first to the baby, so it will be emptied more completely.
- Continue to nurse. If you stop suddenly, the breast is likely to get too full, the condition will be aggravated, and infection may be the result.
- Read the next section, since a clogged duct is sometimes the forerunner of an infection.

BREAST INFECTION (MASTITIS)

Symptoms of a breast infection include headache, painful engorgement, with the breast hot and tender to the touch, redness, fever, and a general sick, ache-y, flu-like feeling. A breast infection is most likely to occur from one to three weeks after delivery and may be a complication of an untreated clogged duct or the result of a staphylococcal infection carried from the baby to the mother. Dr. E. Robbins Kimball, an Illinois pediatrician who has studied and treated many cases of breast infections in nursing mothers, feels they are very often the result of a "lactating indiscretion": not enough rest, too tight a bra, or something else causing a temporary let-up in the let-down reflex.

Mothers with breast infections used to be told to stop nursing immediately. We have found, however, that breast infections clear up more quickly and with fewer complications when the mother continues to nurse from the affected breast. There is no danger of the baby's becoming ill from nursing at an infected breast; he probably harbors the same germs that caused it in his mouth and nose area, anyway.

If a breast infection is treated within twenty-four hours, it is much more likely to heal without developing an abscess. So if you seem to have the symptoms of breast infection, do the following:

- Go to bed immediately and stay there as much as possible.
- Call your doctor right away. He may want to prescribe antibiotics or pain-relievers.
- Apply heat to the affected breast (heating pad, hot water bottle, or hot wet towel).
- Offer the sore breast first at each nursing, so it can be emptied more completely.
- Wear a firm bra for support.

BREAST ABSCESS

An abscess is a localized complication of a general infection, in which pus accumulates in one spot. Antibiotics may heal it, or it may require surgical opening and drainage. If surgery is needed, it can often be done in the doctor's office. Healing is fairly quick. While the breast is healing, nurse the baby on the other side and express or pump milk on the affected side. Throw away this milk. After the abscess is healed, you can resume nursing from that breast.

INSUFFICIENCY OF MILK AFTER ESTABLISHMENT OF SUCCESSFUL NURSING

Many times, your baby will have been happy with a nursing schedule that you and he have worked out, but just as soon as you think you're settled into a routine, he begins to demand more. You wonder what has happened. Where has your milk gone? Why can't you feed him any more? One common answer lies in the fact that nursing has become so easy and apparently so undemanding that you forget to take care of yourself. Your social life becomes active, your housekeeping duties get the better of you, you forget about getting enough rest and a balanced diet. As a result, your milk supply may diminish. This is easy to remedy. Just take a look at your schedule and cut back on some activities. Rest more, eat better, and if necessary, feed the baby a little more often for the next few days.

Another common reason for a sudden insufficiency of milk is related to the fact that babies grow irregularly. During periods of particularly rapid growth, sometimes referred to as "growth spurts," they need more sustenance. The most common times for this apparent increase in need for nourishment seem to come at three weeks, six weeks, three months, and six months. For the first three spurts, probably all you'll have to do is feed the baby more often for a couple of days, until your milk supply increases to meet his demands. (See Chapter Six for ways to increase your milk supply.) Sometime between three and six months, these frequent feedings won't be enough to satisfy the baby, and you'll know that it's time to think about introducing solid foods. Talk to your pediatrician—and take a look at Chapter Ten, which discusses the addition of solid foods to your baby's diet.

THE BABY WHO DOESN'T GAIN

Occasionally a pediatrician sees a baby two or three weeks

old who has gained practically nothing since he went home from the hospital. The baby may be crying constantly, obviously hungry all the time. Or he may sleep for several hours at a stretch, nurse well, and seem happy. Either way, the doctor worries, wondering whether the baby is sick or whether the mother is giving so little milk that the baby is starving.

When a baby is like this, and the mother has been feeding the baby on demand, her doctor may give her suggestions for building up her milk supply and then tell her to wait a few days. If, after four or five days, the baby is still not gaining, an emergency procedure may be advised, with the mother breastfeeding on demand, giving the baby both breasts for five to ten minutes each. Then, she follows each nursing with a bottle of formula, and keeps a written record of how much formula the baby is taking.

After a week of this regime, the doctor sees the baby again. If he is now gaining, both mother and doctor heave a sigh of relief. He is apparently healthy and just needed more to eat. Often the mother, now reassured, is able to build up her milk supply so that the baby takes less and less formula until he is back on breast milk alone. Meanwhile, he will have become more vigorous from these extra feedings during a difficult time for him. Cases like this are usually the only ones for which a supplementary bottle should be recommended. Some other doctors prefer to give solid foods to such a baby—a little mashed banana or even meat—to help him over the rough spots. These cases are rare, fortunately. Should you run into this type of problem, listen carefully to your doctor's advice.

TEMPORARY REJECTION OF THE BREAST

Sometimes, when a baby is somewhere between four and ten months old, he seems to turn against the breast. He'll nurse a couple of minutes and then arch his back and cry piteously. Nothing you can do will induce him to go back to that breast, and yet you can see he wants something. What is wrong? It might be any one of a number of problems.

If you want to continue nursing, don't start to give bottles now. If the baby is eating solid foods, increase his portions of these for a few days. Or if he can drink from a cup, give him his milk that way. Meanwhile, keep on offering the breast. It sometimes helps to completely change your pattern of nursing. If you have been nursing sitting up, try lying down or even standing. Or you might try picking the baby up while he is asleep; he won't remember to reject the breast, and once he is back in the routine, he may decide he wants to stay with it, after all.

Maybe one of the following is causing your baby to reject the breast:

• Teething. If the baby's teeth are bothering him, he may find it painful to nurse. Ask your pediatrician to prescribe something to ease the discomfort of erupting teeth.

• Extreme hunger. Sometimes babies go through stages when they are so wildly hungry that they cannot bear waiting for the milk to let down. When it does not flow immediately, they despair of its ever coming and give up. If this seems to be the problem, try picking the baby up about fifteen minutes before you would ordinarily feed him, to catch him before he realizes how famished he is. Also, try the suggestions given in Chapter Six on how to relax. The more relaxed and rested you are, the faster your milk will let down.

• Bad taste in the milk. Dairymen know that cows who eat garlic give garlic-flavored milk. If you have eaten something not in your regular diet, your gourmet baby may object.

• Emotional Tension. If you are going through a particularly difficult time, your feelings may be communicating themselves to the baby, who in turn becomes too upset to nurse. Make a conscious effort to slough off your cares, cuddle the baby a lot and stay available to him.

• Cold. If your baby is having trouble breathing through his nose, he'll find nursing difficult and may feel it's more trouble than it's worth. Ask your doctor whether nose drops or use of a vaporizer would make his breathing easier.

• Thrush. This fungus infection of the mouth shows up in white, milky-looking spots on the tongue, gums, and insides of the cheeks. It can make nursing painful for the baby. The infection can also spread to the mother, causing sore nipples (See p. 149). When the thrush is treated, both mother and baby are happier. If you think your baby might have it, call your pediatrician.

• If none of these problems apply to your baby and yet, after about a week, he's still refusing the breast, maybe he's telling you that he's ready to be weaned. While some babies don't signal their readiness for weaning till they're strapping toddlers, others seem ready to give up the breast sometime between six and nine months of age. (See Chapter Ten for more about weaning the baby.)

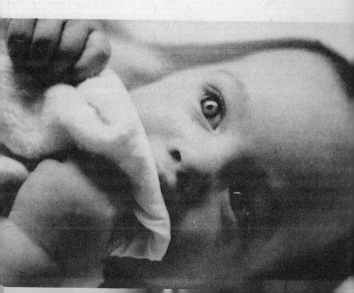

CAESAREAN DELIVERY

If you have your baby by Caesarean section, your breasts will fill up with milk just as soon as if you had given birth by the normal vaginal route. There is no reason at all why you cannot breastfeed successfully. You will probably stay in the hospital a couple of days longer after a Caesarean than if you had delivered normally. And you will need even more rest than the average new mother, both in the hospital and at home. Because of your abdominal incision, you may find it more comfortable to nurse sitting up in a chair; experiment with different positions until you find the one that's easiest for you.

TWINS

The mother of twins doesn't wonder whether to offer one or both breasts at a feeding; she has been designed with perfect efficiency for just this contingency. Breastfeeding twins is *much* more efficient than having to make and store sixteen bottles of formula every day! And since twins are likely to be small, they derive special benefits from breast milk.

You will probably find it easiest to nurse both babies simultaneously for most feedings, even though you will want to nurse them individually occasionally, so that each one will have a chance from time to time to enjoy your undivided attention. And there will be times when one twin is desperately hungry—and the other sound asleep. As a general rule, though, you can try feeding the babies on a modified demand schedule by letting the hungrier twin set the pattern. When you are about to feed him, wake up his brother at the same time. If you let each one set his own schedule, you'll probably be doing nothing else besides feeding babies.

Try to alternate breasts and babies, so that the same twin doesn't always drink at the same fount. But if each baby develops a preference for his own side, don't worry about it.

If one eats more than the other, you may be a little lopsided for the duration of the twins' breastfeeding days, but you'll return to your former evenness when they are weaned.

When breastfeeding twins simultaneously, position is everything. Experiment till you and the babies are comfortable. Find yourself a comfortable armchair and a couple of pillows. Then try one of these:

• Half-recline and lay each baby on his side or stomach lengthwise along your body.

• Sit up and tuck each baby under an arm, heads resting on pillows on your lap and feet by your back.

• Hold one baby on your lap and criss-cross the other across his body.

• Hold one on your lap and tuck the other under your arm.

TRIPLETS

If you're planning to nurse a triple blessing, you'll probably want to prepare one batch of formula a day. Then you can rotate each baby on each breast and the bottle.

JAUNDICE

Many healthy babies develop a yellowish cast to their skin and eyeballs about three or four days after birth. This normal, or physiological, jaundice goes away in about a week. Occasional breastfed babies remain jaundiced, however, for as long as two months. If your baby seems jaundiced, speak to your pediatrician. He will examine the baby, most likely find him in good health, and be able to tell you that his jaundice is perfectly harmless.

Normal jaundice is caused by the immaturity of the baby's liver function. And "breast milk" jaundice seems to be related to the presence in the milk of some mothers of a hormone that interferes with the action of a certain enzyme in the baby's liver. Both these types of jaundice are usually harmless and not symptomatic of any illness. They are completely different from abnormal, or pathological, jaundice caused by a blood incompatibility between mother and baby. A baby with abnormal jaundice, which generally shows up within twenty-four hours of birth, requires close surveillance and careful treatment, but he can almost always still be breastfed.

In the rare case when physiologic or breast milk jaundice is severe, your doctor may want to treat it by exposing your baby to fluorescent light or by giving him small doses of phenobarbital. Or he may want to take the baby off the breast for three or four days, to allow the jaundice to recede. Express your milk during that time, so the baby can resume nursing. Jaundice does not usually become severe again after this brief interruption, and no further treatment is required.

BREASTFEEDING THE PREMATURE INFANT

If your baby is born early, you should still be able to breastfeed him, even though you may have to wait a while before you know the joy of putting him to your breast. Procedures for feeding a premature baby vary, depending on his size, his strength, and his special needs. If he is very tiny, he may not be able to suck at all; he may have to be fed a special high-calorie solution intravenously or through a tube. Or he may be technically classified as premature, but be well-formed and strong and lack only a few ounces to be considered perfectly normal.

Breast milk is usually the best food for the premie, so your premature infant will be lucky indeed if you can supply it for him. Some hospitals, in fact, maintain milk banks of breast milk for those premature babies who need it but cannot get it from their own mothers.

If your baby is too small to nurse at the breast, but you want to breastfeed him later, you should begin to express or pump your breasts the day after delivery. (See the section in this chapter, "Expressing and Keeping Milk.") If the hospital is giving your milk to your baby, you should be expressing every three hours. If you are only interested in maintaining milk production until he is able to nurse, every four hours will be enough.

Many hospitals that used to prevent premature babies from nursing at the breast until they had reached the "normal" weight of five or five and a half pounds, now permit small babies with a strong suck to nurse. So even if your baby has to remain at the hospital after you go home, you may be able to go in every day to nurse him. You will probably be able to take your baby into a special room set aside especially for premature babies and their mothers. If you want to, you may be permitted to stay near your baby all day long, feeding him on demand.

If you cannot do this—either because your baby cannot yet nurse or because you have to be home with other children—you may be able to bring your breast milk to the hospital every day, to be given to your baby in a bottle designed especially for premies. If your own baby isn't getting your milk, you might want to freeze it at home for use in later months, or donate it to a milk bank, if there is one in your community. Even if you just throw away your expressed milk, however, you are not just wasting time. You are maintaining your milk supply in anticipation of that day when you will be able to cradle your baby in your arms and know the happiness of nursing him. One woman who breastfed her premature baby until he was a year and a half old has said, "Breastfeeding a premature baby means a few weeks of uncertainty and inconvenience, followed by many months of blissful happiness, contentment, and satisfaction."

You will find that your premature baby's first few days at home require many adjustments. Used to drinking from a bottle, the baby has to learn to suckle the breast. You may have to take special steps to build up your milk supply to meet his needs (see Chapter Six). Don't let this throw you. If you have had the courage and the persistence to keep up your milk supply all this time, you can certainly manage a few additional adjustments, now that the long-awaited homecoming has arrived. Once the initial adjustment period is over, nursing should go as smoothly for you as if you had nursed your baby right from birth.

However, if you feel that weeks of expressing milk would be too much for you and that you would be able to care for your baby better if you spent this time building up your own strength, don't feel guilty about not breastfeeding. Remember that feeding your baby at the breast is one wonderful way to show your love for your baby, but it is not the only way. Many premature babies thrive beautifully on formula. And you can still hold and cuddle your baby when you feed him with a bottle.

ILLNESS OF THE MOTHER

With most types of illness, a nursing mother can continue to breastfeed. However, should you develop such symptoms of illness as fever, vomiting, or diarrhea, call your pediatrician, and if the symptoms persist for twenty-four hours, call your own doctor.

FATIGUE IN THE MOTHER

Breastfeeding is a perfectly normal physiological function and there is no reason for blaming a new mother's exhaustion on the fact that she is nursing her baby. Some women never break stride through pregnancy, childbirth, and lactation, while others find enormous strain in some or all stages of the reproductive process. If you are so tired that you "just can't take it," don't give up breastfeeding. Give up trying to do too much in the house or out of it. Eat well. Rest often. Pamper yourself. Best of all, make the most of those relaxing nursing sessions.

SKIN RASH ON THE BABY

If your baby's skin becomes reddened or rough while he is getting nothing but breast milk, you need not worry about allergy, since no baby is allergic to his mother's milk. An occasional nursing baby does, however, show some reddening of the buttocks, probably because of the high acidity of the nursling's feces. This type of perianal irritation is nothing to worry about; it should go away in a few days if you expose the baby's buttocks to the air and put some type of lubrication on the affected area. If a rash persists more than twenty-four hours or suddenly becomes severe, call your doctor. It is always best to catch a skin disorder as soon as possible, instead of letting it go on to make the baby miserable.

FORCED SEPARATION
OF THE NURSING COUPLE

Occasionally, emergencies come up that separate a breast-feeding mother and her baby for a period of days or weeks. If you want to continue nursing past this separation, it can be done. If you want to wean the baby before the separation, plan ahead, if possible, so that you can do it gradually.

If the separation is caused by the baby's hospitalization, you may be able to obtain permission to stay with him during his hospital stay and to continue nursing him. Many progressive hospitals permit parents to stay with young children, in recognition of the emotional support the children need. If this is impossible, you may still be able to visit the baby several times a day and nurse him then. If you are not able to see the baby at all, you can still continue to express your milk at the times you would ordinarily be nursing, and resume breastfeeding when your baby returns home.

If you must be hospitalized, and if your condition permits, you may be able to have your baby come to stay with you in the hospital. If this is impossible, ask your doctor to leave orders for your breasts to be pumped regularly during your hospital stay, so that you can resume nursing when you go home. Meanwhile, you may be able to find another nursing mother who will feed your baby while you are away. (Your pediatrician or local La Leche League leader may know someone who would be willing to help you this way.) If not, your baby can be fed by bottle while you are gone.

EXPRESSING AND KEEPING MILK

Throughout this book, we have referred to situations when you might want to express or pump and then store your breast milk. Instructions for hand-expression are given in Chapter Four. The two other methods involve pumping, by hand or electric pump.

HAND PUMP

You can buy an inexpensive hand breast pump in the drugstore. But many a nursing mother has decided that it is easier to find one than to use it. However, if you want to try to pump your milk this way, this is how you do it.

The pump consists of a glass cup attached to a rubber bulb. Place the glass part against your breast and squeeze the rubber bulb rhythmically. The milk will come out from the breast and into a little bubble on the bottom of the glass cup. When the bubble is full, empty the milk into a container. Sterilize the pump after every use.

ELECTRIC PUMP

Electric breast pumps are quite expensive, costing almost $300, but they can often be rented for about $25 a month. If you are going to be pumping milk for any length of time, the rental of an electric pump is a worthwhile investment. Many hospitals keep them on hand. And some local La Leche League chapters lend them out free to women in special circumstances. Before you rent one, find out whether there is one in your community that you might borrow.

The two pumps in common use are the Egnell pump, made in Sweden, and the Gomco pump. The Egnell more closely imitates the suckling action of a nursing baby, but the Gomco's suction action seems to be just as effective in drawing out the milk and it is more readily available.

Whichever pump you obtain will come with directions for operating it and regulating the degree of sucking action to your own comfort.

Start by pumping only two or three minutes on each breast; then gradually build up until you are pumping for about ten to fifteen minutes on each breast. Switch breasts several times during the course of the pumping; you get more milk out this way. If you are pumping one breast only, you will empty it more completely if you use the pump while you are nursing the baby on your other breast. The baby produces the let-down reflex on the breast being pumped as well as on the one being suckled.

STORING THE MILK

If you are going to store milk to be taken to the hospital for a sick or premature baby, for donation to a milk bank, or for future use, you will want to express and store it in a sterile container. If the milk is to be given to your baby in your home within forty-eight hours, it can go into a thoroughly washed, unsterilized container and put in the refrigerator.

If you have a dishwasher that uses 180° water, this will sterilize your equipment well enough. Before putting baby equipment in the dishwasher or sterilizing it, be sure it is clean and free from any milk scum. Use a bottle brush on the inside of the bottle and a nipple brush in the inside of the nipple.

To sterilize just a few things, fill a pot with enough water to completely cover the items you are sterilizing (bottle, cup, bottle caps, nipples, funnel, etc.). Bring the water to a boil over high heat; then turn down the heat just enough so that the water continues to boil gently. After five minutes of boiling, remove the nipples with sterile tongs. Place them on a clean towel. Allow the other items to boil fifteen minutes longer. Do not touch the rims of the bottles or the insides of the caps.

If you want to keep the milk longer than forty-eight hours, freeze it. Milk will keep for two weeks in the freezing compartment of a single-door refrigerator, for several months in the $0°$ freezer of a two-door refrigerator, and up to a couple of years in the back or bottom of a deep-freeze unit.

To defrost frozen milk, move it from the freezer to the refrigerator a few hours before it is to be used. Then, when you plan to feed it to the baby, hold the bottle for a few minutes under running tap water that is about as warm as body temperature. (If you try to thaw it out too quickly in boiling water, the milk will curdle.) When the milk is defrosted, shake it up to homogenize it, since the cream will probably have risen to the top. The amount of cream in the milk will vary depending on the time of day you expressed the milk; some feedings are creamier than others.

RH INCOMPATIBILITY

If you have Rh negative blood, you can still breastfeed your Rh positive baby. The Rh factor is a certain protein substance carried in the red blood cells of about 85% of the population. Persons who have this factor in their blood are considered Rh positive; those without it are considered Rh negative. It sometimes happens that during pregnancy or, more commonly, during labor and delivery, the blood of the unborn baby penetrates the placenta and enters the mother's circulatory system. When this happens in the case of an Rh negative mother and an Rh positive infant, antibodies build up in the mother's blood to fight the Rh factor as a foreign substance. The mother is then sensitized against the Rh factor; should she become pregnant with another Rh positive baby, the antibodies now in her system will attack the red blood cells of the fetus, possibly causing miscarriage or stillbirth, or anemia or jaundice in the newborn. Many infants with Rh disease are cured by having all their blood replaced with healthy Rh negative blood immediately after birth, or even through intrauterine transfusion during the two months before birth. Some infants require more than one exchange transfusion.

Today, Rh negative women who have not already been sensitized to the Rh factor do not have to fear that their babies will be affected by Rh disease. A new vaccine can now be administered routinely to every Rh negative woman within seventy-two hours after the birth of an Rh positive infant, to prevent the mother's blood from forming antibodies against the Rh factor.

The vaccine itself contains antibodies, which remain temporarily in the mother's body. A few of them do pass through the milk but do not cause any harm, since those that reach the baby in this way are broken down by his stomach enzymes and thus prevented from attacking his red blood cells.

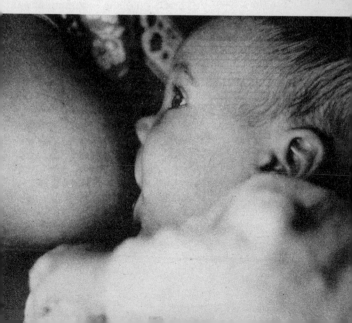

If you have already been sensitized to the Rh factor, you can still breastfeed your baby—even if he has been affected by Rh disease. If the infant has only a mild case, there is no problem at all; breastfeeding can take its normal course from birth. The baby who has had to be completely transfused can usually be back at the breast within six hours after the blood replacement.

In the rare case of a severely affected infant who has received an exchange transfusion and then is still so sick that he requires intensive care therapy and constant surveillance, breastfeeding may have to be postponed for a short time as it would for a small premature infant. However, if the mother is willing to express or pump her milk until the baby is well enough to nurse normally, there is no reason why this baby should have to be deprived of the ideal infant food—his mother's milk.

BREAST CANCER

If you have a history of breast cancer in your family, you will be interested in knowing about the most recent research findings in this area, particularly as they pertain to breast feeding.

Since the 1930s, extensive research has been carried out with laboratory mice in an effort to find the cause of mammary cancer. Special strains of mice were bred, with either a very high or a very low susceptibility to mammary tumors. A specific particle was discovered in the milk of some of these mice and identified as a cancer-producing virus. The virus particles were also found in the genitalia of male mice, and it was established that the father mouse, too, could pass this virus on to his offspring. Most commonly, however, the virus is transmitted from mother to daughter. Further research disclosed that when mouse pups from the high-cancer strain were nursed by mothers from the low-cancer strain, they were less likely to develop mammary cancer, and vice versa. Therefore, researchers concluded that virus particles passed through the milk seemed to be capable of inducing breast cancer in female mice. Not all the female mice who carried this virus developed cancer, however. Genetic and hormonal factors were apparently influential in determining which mice developed mammary cancer.

Recently, virus-like particles similar to those isolated in the milk of mice have been identified in the milk of some women. Fairly limited studies have disclosed that women with a family history of breast cancer are more likely to show evidence of these particles in their milk. Because of the similarities between the mouse particles and the human particles, doctors are investigating the possibility that breast cancer in humans may also be caused by a virus. They are also trying to find out the means of transmission of the disease, and they hope eventually to develop a vaccine against this form of cancer.

While much of our knowledge about bacterial and viral infections has been founded on work with laboratory animals, it is dangerous to assume that scientific conclusions related to animals may always be applied to human beings. People do not necessarily react the way laboratory animals do. And in these particular experiments the mice involved had been highly bred by twenty or more brother-sister matings, so that their general constitution was radically altered from that of the normal mouse.

At the moment, then, we are not even positive that those particles found in human milk are cancer-producing viruses. And even if further research should point to the conclusion that these viruses are related to breast cancer and are passed on to infants through their mothers' milk, it would still leave unanswered two important questions: Why is it that not every woman with these particles in her milk develops breast cancer? And why is the rate of breast cancer lower in populations where infants are routinely nursed than it is in societies where artificial feeding is more popular?

In short, we can refer to a statement by one physician who has for many years been involved in this research.* Michael J. Brennan, M.D., President and Scientific Director of the Michigan Cancer Foundation, says, "The woman with a family history of breast cancer has to balance the very doubtful evidence that breast cancer risk for her daughter will be increased to some modest degree if the child is nursed, against the known nutritional, immunological and psychological benefits that breastfeeding will give this child throughout her developmental years.

"So far," concludes Dr. Brennan, "there is nothing in medical knowledge or historical experience to tell women, including women with a family history of breast cancer, not to nurse their babies."

Some physicians, in fact, urge women with such a history to nurse their babies, in the belief that it is possible that giving birth to several children and nursing them for extended periods may decrease a woman's likelihood of developing cancer of the breast. This belief has stemmed largely from the knowledge that in most of the countries with low rates of breast cancer, lactation is both customary and prolonged; that the more children a woman has, the less likely she is to develop cancer of the breast; and that the significant increase of breast cancer among relatively young women in the United States in recent years has seemed to parallel the fall from popularity of breastfeeding in this country.

Several studies in the past have indicated that women who have developed cancer of the breast have either nursed their children less frequently or for shorter periods of time than comparable groups of women without such disease.

* The studies being carried on in this field of research are dependent for their results on obtaining samples of breast milk, especially from women with a family history of breast cancer. Nursing mothers who wish to help in research that may ultimately yield a vaccine against breast cancer are urged to contact their local cancer society or Dr. Brennan at the Michigan Cancer Foundation, 4811 John-R Street, Detroit, Michigan.

However, the 1970 reports of an extensive study conducted in seven different countries under the auspices of the World Health Organization concluded that there were no consistent differences in the duration of lactation between breast cancer patients and unaffected women, once the factor of fewer pregnancies among the cancer patients had been accounted for.

Those doctors who still consider breastfeeding a protection against breast cancer point to circumstantial evidence, such as the fact that women of pure Japanese extraction living in California are three times more likely to develop breast cancer than women living in Japan, and women in America are less likely to breastfeed than are women living in Japan. Also, Canadian Eskimo women, who have large families and nurse all their babies for two or three years, appear to have the lowest rate of breast cancer of any group. Only one case of breast cancer has ever been proved among these women—and that occurred in a mother who nursed her babies on only one breast, because the nipple on the affected breast "did not work."

If breastfeeding does prevent breast cancer, possible explanations might be in the changes of hormonal balance in the body of the nursing woman, including the fact that she has fewer menstrual cycles throughout her lifetime, or the possibility that suppressing the normal process of lactation may encourage abnormal development of mammary cells.

Until all the evidence is in on this topic, no definite conclusions can be drawn, other than to state that *if there is any relationship at all between the two phenomena, it is in the direction of lactation's preventing breast cancer in the mother—and certainly not causing it.*

As to the effect of nursing on the child's risk of developing the disease, Dr. Brennan reaffirms, "Since there is literally no direct evidence to date that the risk is increased with respect to breast cancer, no medical reason against breastfeeding exists."

RELACTATION AND NURSING AN ADOPTED BABY

Most people are surprised to learn that a woman who is not currently lactating can stimulate her breasts to produce milk, either for her own baby who may have developed a digestive problem requiring breast milk, or for a baby she has adopted. This is not easy, but it is possible. Women who have never been pregnant or who have not been pregnant for years have been able to stimulate their breasts to produce milk for adopted babies.

If you have given your baby a formula right from birth, or if you have weaned him completely, and then, several months later, you find that there is some compelling reason for him to go back to the breast—a digestive or allergic problem, for example—or if you want to nurse an adopted baby, you may be able to produce milk. Do not go into this thinking it will be a simple matter. You must be willing to persevere for several months, to nurse almost constantly around the clock for the first few weeks to bring in the milk, and to supplement your baby's diet with formula. If you have lactated before, you may be able to build up enough milk to nourish your baby on that alone. If not, he will probably continue to need formula feedings, as well as the breast feedings.

Mrs. Elizabeth Hormann, a Massachusetts mother who breastfed an adopted baby after nursing two of her own children, studied twenty-seven cases in which mothers who had not recently been pregnant or who had never been pregnant were able to establish lactation. Several of the women prepared to breastfeed before they received their babies through extensive regimes of hand expression or electric pumping, which helped to bring in the milk. In a few cases, certain drugs seemed to facilitate lactation. The average time for establishing the baby's total milk supply from the breast ranged from two and a half to five months. By this time, either the mother had a full milk supply or she was substituting solid food for supplementary formula.

All twenty-seven mothers in this group nursed their babies for at least six weeks, most for longer. Mrs. Hormann found that "nearly all the babies were taking considerably less formula than expected for their size and age. The assumption was that nursing supplied the rest." All the mothers believed they had closer ties to their babies because of the nursing experience. Mrs. Hormann went on to caution, however, that relactation "should never be casually suggested, especially to adoptive mothers. Unless a mother is properly motivated and very carefully prepared for this experience, it can lead to grievous disappointment in her baby and herself."

One adoptive father, John Avery, has invented an ingenious device called the Nursing Supplementer, which his wife used to nurse their adopted baby. It has also been used by other mothers in adoptive and other relactation situations. The appliance consists of a collapsible plastic bag into which formula is poured, a lid, and a long, very thin tube. The bag fits into the mother's nursing bra between her breasts and the tube is placed next to her nipple. The infant suckles the breast and the tube simultaneously, receiving milk as soon as he starts to nurse. The Nursing Supplementer seems to help a mother in her efforts to establish lactation, since her baby has no opportunity to get used to a bottle and since her breasts receive strong stimulation. The greater value of the device, however, may lie in its ability to provide both mother and baby with the experience of nursing *at* the breast, if not *by* the breast, in situations where supplementation is necessary. For more information about the Nursing Supplementer, contact Mrs. Jimmie Lynne Avery, P.O. Box 6459, Denver, Colorado 80206.

While the strongly motivated woman who is willing to invest a considerable amount of time and effort may reap the rewards of nursing an adopted baby, in most cases the adoptive mother would probably be better advised to show her love for her baby in other ways.

If you do want information and counseling in relactation, contact La Leche League, Mrs. Avery, or Mrs. Hormann (One Merrill Avenue, Belmont, Massachusetts 02178).

THE WORKING NURSING MOTHER

You may plan to go back to work after your baby is born, to combine motherhood with a professional career. If so, you will not be alone. In 1969, more than two million mothers of children under three were in the labor force— some twenty-five per cent of all women in this category. Some women pursue their professions by choice, though the great majority work because of pressing financial need. Your decision as to how long you should stay home will be a very personal one, based on your physical stamina and ability to combine the demands of this double life; your economic circumstances; your commitment to a profession; and your feelings about the importance of being home with your young children. You may want to defer resumption of your career until all your children are in school, or you may wait only until each baby is sleeping through the night and you are feeling back to your old self again.

You will find it much easier to be a working mother if you can cut your schedule back to part-time while your children are young. This is a happy solution for many women, permitting them to pursue their careers, keep up with their professions, earn a little extra money, and still have enough time with their children to enjoy the rewards of motherhood. Nursing a baby while working is, or course, much easier if you work part-time, either at home or nearby.

By the time the average breastfed baby is three or four months old, he will have worked out a fairly regular schedule for his feedings. If you do the type of work that can be performed at home or if you have a flexible schedule, you should be able to fit all the baby's feedings around your work schedule, just as you would if you were a full-time homemaker.

If, on the other hand, you want to (or have to) go back to work outside the home full-time, you may still be able to continue breastfeeding. You can feed the baby in the morning before you leave, feed him in the evening as soon as you come home, and then again around 10 P.M. if he is still taking a late evening feeding. About midway through your working day, you can go into the ladies' room and express some milk, both to alleviate your own discomfort and to keep up your milk production. If there is a refrigerator where you work, you can express this milk into a sterile container and save it to be given to the baby the next day. Otherwise, he can have formula for his noon meal.

As a working mother, you will have a special appreciation of the joys of breastfeeding. Even though you are away from your baby during the day, you will know the warmth and intimacy of the nursing relationship when you are home. It will help you both to make up for the hours when you are apart. And can you think of a nicer way to come home at night than to sink into a comfortable chair, put up your feet, and know the peace and serenity of nursing your baby?

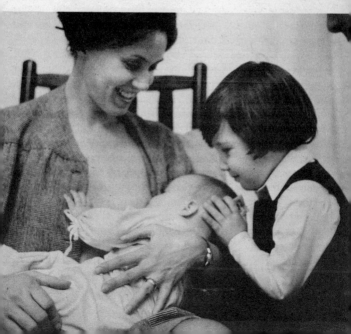

CHAPTER 10.

WEANING THE BABY

Weaning is the process by which a baby stops depending on his mother's milk for nourishment. Strictly speaking, then, you *begin* to wean your child as soon as you give him any food at all besides breast milk: that first relief bottle of formula or those first few spoonfuls of applesauce. Your baby is fully weaned when he no longer nurses at the breast, but gets all his food from other sources. But before we talk about complete weaning, let's discuss some of your baby's other nourishment needs.

OTHER ELEMENTS OF YOUR BABY'S DIET

VITAMIN DROPS

Most of your baby's vitamins will come from the grocery and not from the drugstore—that is, from the foods that you eat, and later from those he will eat—rather than from vitamin drops or pills. There are some elements, though, that cannot always be obtained in the diet. For this reason, your doctor will probably prescribe specific vitamin supplements for your baby, to be taken through the first year of life. Most pediatricians prescribe a multiple vitamin preparation that contains the vitamins D, C and A.

It is particularly important for your baby to receive extra vitamin D, which helps the body absorb calcium and phosphorus, essential elements for bone and tooth growth and development. Babies who are growing rapidly need especially large amounts of this vitamin, which appears in only tiny amounts in any food, including breast milk. Vitamin D is called the "sunshine" vitamin, since it is manufactured by our bodies when we spend a great deal of time outdoors and expose our bodies to sunlight. Most children, especially those

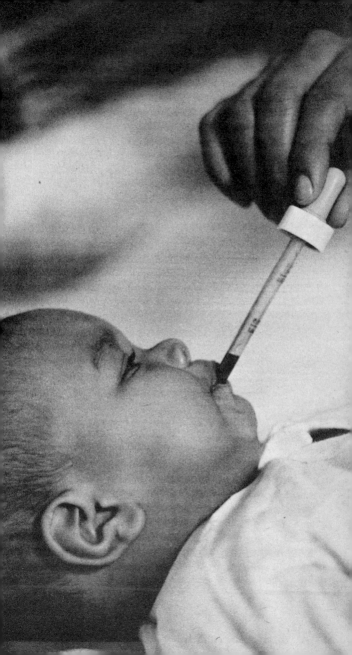

who live in cold climates, can't depend on the amount they get from sunshine, however, and need extra vitamin D at least until adolescence. This can come either through vitamin drops or specially fortified milk.

Vitamin A and C are two other factors important for body growth and functioning. If you yourself are eating fruits and vegetables rich in these vitamins, your baby will probably get enough of them through your milk. But just to be sure that his needs are fully met, your doctor will most likely prescribe them in the form of drops.

You can now get this triple vitamin preparation fortified with iron. Neither cow's milk nor breast milk contains more than a trace of this essential mineral. Since recent studies have found that some babies who do not receive extra iron tend to become anemic between the ages of eight and twelve months, The American Academy of Pediatrics now recommends extra iron for all babies during their first year.

If you live in a community without fluoridation of the water supply, your pediatrician may prescribe a preparation that contains vitamins, iron, *and* fluoride. Children who drink fluoridated water from birth are likely to have up to 65% fewer cavities than those who do not; children who live in communities with unfluoridated water can receive the benefits of fluoride by having it added to their diet. Even if your water is fluoridated, your baby may need the extra fluoride if he does not drink much water. Studies have shown that the fluoride in the water drunk by a nursing mother does not pass through the milk in sufficient amounts to help her baby develop decay-resistant teeth.

COW'S MILK

If you have had any thoughts at all about weaning your baby from the breast before he is completely trained to the cup, you have probably been offering him an occasional bottle since he was under two months of age. If these bottles contained breast milk, it is an easy matter to substitute cow's milk.

A baby who is several months old and has never had a bottle will by mystified by the strange contraption the first time around and may absolutely refuse to try sucking the rubber nipple. If you have not been giving your baby an occasional bottle since he was two months old or so, be prepared for a difficult period when he is likely to reject the bottle completely.

To avoid the baby's developing this kind of resistance to the cup, you should start offering him a few sips of milk from a cup at about five months. By the time he's really ready for it, he'll be quite proficient at draining it to the last drop.

Important note: If you have a history of allergy in your family, you may want to avoid cow's milk as long as possible. The later a baby is given a potentially allergenic food, the less likely he is to react against it. So if you think your baby might have inherited a tendency to allergy, give breast milk only in the early relief bottles. Try cow's milk at about six months; if your baby shows an allergic response, such as diarrhea, vomiting, or marked irritability, you will know that in your case especially, it will be advisable to feed him on breast milk alone for a while longer, and to be very careful about any additions to his diet.

SOLID FOODS

Virtually all babies need some form of solid food added to the diet by the time they are six months old and sometimes earlier. Breast milk is an ideal food for the young infant but it must be supplemented with other foods for the older baby, since breast milk alone does not continue to meet all his nutritional requirements. The precise age at which each baby needs additional foods varies, usually ranging between three and eight months.

There is no evidence at all, however, that feeding solid food to very young infants (except in very special circumstances) serves any purpose other than to gratify the competitive drives of their mothers. Many women feel they have to be the first on their block to shovel baby food into their children's mouths, sometimes feeding infants a week old from a spoon! Too early a rush to feed a baby solid foods may produce allergies. It may also fill him up so much that he nurses less vigorously, bringing about a decrease in his mother's milk supply. In addition, it may be a form of over-feeding that creates fat babies who turn into obese adults. Aside from being unnecessary and possibly injurious, early feeding of solid foods is a waste of your time and your money.

How, then, will you know when to introduce solid foods into your baby's diet? If, at some time after three months, your baby seems to show by frequent crying that he is not satisfied with the breast milk alone, despite more frequent nursings for a few days, he probably needs something extra added to his diet. If he has not shown this increased appetite by the age of six months, you should introduce solids at this time. Six months seems to be the point at which human beings need additional foods in their diet. Babies of under-nourished women, for example, often grow beautifully on breast milk alone for the first six months. Once they pass this crucial time, however, they fall ill with a variety of diseases caused by malnutrition.

INTRODUCING SOLID FOODS

Cereal or fruit is likely to be your baby's first semi-solid food— cereal because it is filling or fruit because babies like its taste. Vegetables, meat, and eggs will follow later. It is very important to introduce only one new food at a time. Occasionally a baby will show an allergic reaction to a new food—hives, a diaper rash, or a stomach upset—and if you introduce two different new foods within a couple of days of each other, you will not be able to identify the one causing the trouble. So wait two to three days after giving one new food before offering something else.

When you give your baby cereal, you can mix it with a little bit of homogenized milk. Small amounts of whole milk are generally well accepted by babies old enough to be eating solid foods.

Nurse your baby first before you offer him his spoon-feedings. He will be more likely to try a new experience if he is not wildly hungry and denied his usual routine. Consider these first few feedings of solids "practice feeds," just like those first few nursings. Your baby has to learn how to master a completely new set of muscle movements to take the food from a spoon and to swallow it. At first, he'll get more food on his face, his bib, and you than he will in his mouth. You'll be surprised, though, at how quickly he catches on.

Use a demitasse spoon, if you already have one, for the baby's early feedings. If not, you can buy an inexpensive

long-handled spoon with a small bowl designed especially for feeding an infant. You're likely to find one in the five and dime or supermarket.

If your baby sits up well, you can feed him in his high chair. If not, put him in an infant seat that permits him to half-recline or hold him slightly tilted back in your lap, with one of his arms tucked under yours. (This will help to prevent him from knocking the food-laden spoon out of your hand.) As soon as the baby opens his mouth, put the spoon with a tiny bit of food on it on the center of his tongue—not so far back that you make him gag but not so far front that he can easily spit it out. Draw the spoon out, wiping the food on the bottom of his upper lip. Eventually he will learn how to move the food from his lip and his tongue into his throat.

COMMERCIAL OR HOMEMADE FOODS?

Once your baby has made the progression from cereal to fruit to vegetables to meat and eggs, he can have as varied a diet as anyone else in the family. You should pay as much attention to the balance of his meals as you do your own, seeing that he has an ample supply of foods with high nutritional value. You should not overload a baby with starchy foods or sweets, just as you should not overload yourself with these foods.

An easy way to provide a balanced diet is to take advantage of the many strained baby foods on your grocer's shelves. These are prepared under strict hygienic conditions and are extremely convenient to use. They are quite expensive, however, for the amount of food you get. In fact, baby foods have been estimated to cost more, in terms of food ounce per dollar, than a good steak. The commercial baby foods have a high water content, and they often contain ingredients that your baby does not need, such as sugar, salt, and a starch thickener.

You can probably offer your baby a better diet for less money if you get yourself a blender and prepare his foods yourself until he is able to eat table food. While you're preparing baby's portion, you can keep the seasonings and sweetenings minimal or nonexistent. The money you save in one month of not buying baby foods can pay for your blender.

If, however, you hate to cook and would resent spending the extra time in the kitchen pureeing foods for your baby, stick to the commercial foods. You'll be less likely to pressure your baby into eating "the good foods Mommy made for you" and better able to enjoy his feeding times. A few words of caution about baby foods: Be sure you hear a pop when you unscrew the lid of the jar; if you don't hear this sound, the vacuum seal has been broken and the food may be contaminated. Do not feed your baby directly from the jar unless he finishes the entire jar at one sitting; the saliva carried back to the food on the spoon can spoil the rest of the food. Immediately refrigerate the unused contents of a jar; after forty-eight hours, throw out whatever is left.

Your baby's food may seem quite bland and tasteless to you. It should. Babies do not care about and should not have seasonings added to their food. Baby food manufacturers used to add monosodium glutamate and considerable amounts of salt to improve the flavor of their products—not because the babies seemed to know the difference, but only because the mothers did. In light of recent findings about possible harmful effects of these additives, MSG has been eliminated from baby food and its salt content has been reduced.

When you prepare family meals, try to remove the baby's portion before you add the seasonings. Once your baby is eating a variety of foods, he can eat (in a pureed form, if necessary) anything the rest of the family eats, if it is not highly salted, sweetened, or spiced. Some good early semi-solid foods are applesauce, mashed ripe banana, cottage cheese, yogurt, pureed stewed or canned fruits, cooked vegetables, and mashed sweet or white potatoes.

When your baby sits up well, you can put on his tray a variety of foods that he can pick up with his fingers. He may play with them and enjoy mashing them, but he will eventually put them in his mouth and be on his way to eating regular table foods. Again, introduce only one new food at a time. If the baby has had the food in its baby-food counterpart, you don't have to consider it new. Otherwise, wait a few days before offering any other new item. Some good early finger foods are pieces of banana; pared apple, pear, or peach; cubes of cheddar or Swiss cheese; slices of cooked carrots; cooked peas and green beans; crusts of whole-wheat bread; bagels; anise toast; pieces of cooked hamburger; flaked cooked fish; and good-sized bones with some meat on them. Avoid ketchup and mustard, carbonated beverages, chocolate, and sweet cookies and cakes.

WHEN SHOULD YOU WEAN YOUR BABY?

As a breastfeeding mother, you are probably used to being asked questions as soon as people find out you are nursing. The first one is usually "Why are your breastfeeding?" And the second is often "How long are you going to keep it up?" There is no reason why you have to set an advance deadline on the duration of breastfeeding, any more than you set a date well ahead of time for the length of time you plan to wheel your baby in his stroller—or put him to sleep in a crib—or diaper him at bedtime. You will stop breastfeeding when the time seems right for weaning your baby.

Weaning customs vary considerably around the world. In many countries, babies are routinely nursed well into the second and sometimes even into the third year of life. In a World Health Organization publication, Dr. Derrick B. Jelliffe states that, at least in tropical and subtropical countries, "prolonged breast feeding through the first two years of life is undoubtedly a measure of great importance and value and must be encouraged in every possible way." On the other hand, in a recent article in a medical journal, Dr. Ronald MacKeith urged doctors to encourage mothers to breastfeed for at least the first two months. For the most part, in the United States and some other western countries, mothers plan to wean their babies from the breast at some time between six and nine months.

There are some good reasons for the popularity of this weaning time. At six months of age, the baby in a modern industrialized society can meet his nutritional needs through cow's milk and a wide variety of solid foods. Breast milk is still good for him, of course, but it is not so important to his physical development as it was when it provided his only source of nourishment. After nine months, a nursing mother usually produces less milk and her let-down reflex takes longer to operate. The anthropologist Ashley Montagu theorizes that human babies are born only half-done—that half of their gestation takes place in the womb and the other half outside it. This "extrauterine gestation" comes to an end at about nine months of age, when a baby can crawl around after food, has several teeth to chew it with and has the intestinal maturity to handle a diversity of foodstuffs. He is still, of course, overwhelmingly dependent on his mother for the essentials of life, but, from a nutritional aspect, he need not be dependent on her milk.

The emotional benefits that a mother and baby derive from breastfeeding are just as valid, however, at nine months or a year or even later. You are still maintaining a special intimate relationship with your baby, still able to comfort him at the breast when he is sick or unhappy, still able to forget the cares of the day for those precious minutes while the two of you are a nursing couple. If you want to continue nursing for psychological reasons rather than nutritional ones, there is no need to stop at any specified time. On the other hand, if you want to stop nursing after only three or four months, you need not feel apologetic. Even if you have nursed only a few weeks and you have to or want to stop breastfeeding, don't consider yourself a failure. You have given your baby a good start in life and you have known the special joy of the nursing relationship. A little breastfeeding is better than none at all.

How, then, do you decide when to wean? Remember that

you and your baby together constitute the nursing couple; the feelings of each of you should be considered. You may not have had any thoughts at all of weaning your baby when suddenly—say at about seven months—he signals his readiness for giving up the breast. He may completely reject it and refuse to nurse, no matter what inducements you offer (see "Temporary Rejection of the Breast" in Chapter Nine). Or he may nurse eagerly for a minute or two and then—just as soon as your milk lets down—pull away and show no further interest. Or you may have a jolly gymnast on your hands—a baby who starts to stand up while nursing, then shows off some of his other acrobatic tricks. Babies who act in these ways are often letting their mothers know that they are ready to say goodbye to their nursing days.

Suppose that your baby has shown no signs of giving up the breast, but you are restless. The baby eagerly takes an occasional relief bottle, eats healthy portions of solid food and even drinks a little milk from a cup. You have resumed some of your former activities and are beginning to resent the time you spend breastfeeding. When you feel this way, it is time to start weaning your baby. Why spoil the months of happy breastfeeding by continuing to nurse because you feel it is your duty? Your resentment and impatience will communicate themselves to the baby. You will be able to provide far better mothering to him if you feel happy and comfortable with what you are doing. It is better for a baby to drink a bottle happily than nurse at a grudging breast, just as it is better for a baby to be cared for by a warm, affectionate babysitter than by a restless, unhappy mother who would rather be at work.

Suppose you would really like to breastfeed your baby past his first or even his second birthday, but are embarrassed by the idea. (Is it any worse for a toddler to be nursing than it is for him to be carrying around a bottle?) You may wonder whether late nursing may make a child too dependent on his mother. There have not been any studies testing a child's degree of independence as related to time of weaning; even if

At one year: still a nursing couple

there were, there would be so many other variables present that it would be impossible to establish a relationship between the two. From our observations, children who have been nursed as toddlers do not seem to be any different from children who have been weaned earlier. Provided the mother-child relationship is warm and loving, the length of breast-feeding—or even, the fact of breastfeeding itself—does not seem to be an all-important factor in the child's healthy psychological development.

You should feel free to answer people who ask, "What? *Still* nursing?" as well as those who exclaim "You gave up *already?*" with a brief statement indicating that you feel this is a decision every mother should make for herself.

You should *not* start to wean your baby when he has other adjustments to make. If he is unhappy because of teething or a cold, or if you have just moved to a new home, or if there is some other disruption of his usual routine, put off the weaning for a few weeks. If possible, it is always best to confront children with one adjustment at a time.

HOW SHOULD YOU WEAN THE BABY?

There may not be a right time to wean, but there is definitely a right way—gradually and sympathetically. Weaning is a natural process; the natural way to help it along is to do it little by little, over a period of some weeks. Slow, gradual weaning is much less of a wrench—both physically and emotionally—for both you and your baby.

Once you have made your decision to wean, try to pinpoint the nursing session in which your baby is least interested. It will probably be the early evening or noontime feeding. Eliminate this one first, substituting a bottle if the baby is less than a year old. Most babies enjoy sucking on a bottle until they are well past a year—some till they are two or three. If your baby doesn't show any interest in the bottle, though, don't try to force him to take one. Not all babies find bottles appealing.

After a week or two, eliminate the next lightest feeding

Not all babies find bottles appealing

of the day. Keep doing this until you are down to one feeding a day, probably the first one of the morning or the last one at night. By now, you will be producing very little milk and your baby will probably give up this last feeding easily. Weaning this way should take from a couple of weeks to a couple of months.

If you wean slowly like this, you should have little or no discomfort from milk pressure; you will gradually produce less and less milk until there is virtually none at all. If at any point in the weaning process, the pressure of your milk makes you uncomfortable, you can put the baby to the breast for a minute or two, or express just enough milk to ease your discomfort. Don't overdo it, or you'll just encourage the breasts to keep producing copious amounts of milk.

Try to make yourself especially available to your baby while he is being weaned. Since he is losing something he has valued greatly—the pleasure of suckling at your breast—he should not be losing your company, as well. If you can temporarily spend extra time with him, this will be reassuring. If you make a special effort to give him foods he is particularly fond of, he will not miss your breast milk so much. Don't ever feel guilty or apologetic about weaning your baby; you are helping him in his first steps toward independence. But be aware that he is making an adjustment. Your loving understanding can help him make it more smoothly.

Fortunately, we don't hear about women in our society resorting to such drastic weaning measures as painting their breasts with pepper or soot, tactics that have been practiced by mothers through the years to discourage their babies from nursing. Most nursing mothers today want breastfeeding to end just as smoothly and happily as possible, unmarred by the psychologic jolts of such stratagems.

SUDDEN WEANING

Sometimes a situation comes up that requires abrupt weaning—a serious illness of the mother, for example, or some other emergency. Such a situation is somewhat analogous to drying up the milk right after childbirth, except for the fact that a woman who has been breastfeeding will have more milk. If you absolutely have to wean suddenly, you'll have to expect to experience considerable discomfort for several days unless you are producing very little milk. You can relieve it somewhat by expressing just enough milk to ease the pressure in your breasts. Your doctor may prescribe a hormonal preparation to speed the drying-up process, and he may also recommend that you restrict your fluids and bind your breasts. Applications of heat may also bring relief.

YOUR FEELINGS ABOUT WEANING

When you stop breastfeeding, you will undergo certain

physiological changes. The hormonal balance in your body will shift, returning to what it was before you became pregnant. Your breasts will change again. It may take three or four months for you to lose all of your milk, even though none may be apparent within days after the last nursing session. It may also take several months for your breasts to return to their former size. They will most likely be less firm than they were before you became pregnant, but, as we pointed out earlier, this is the result of childbearing, not breastfeeding. An occasional woman is convinced that her breasts are smaller after breastfeeding than they had been before she became pregnant. She may have become so accustomed to her more bosomy state during pregnancy and nursing that she has forgotten her true size. Or she may have lost weight in the intervening time, with the result that she has less fatty tissue in the breasts. The majority of women find no change in breast size after nursing.

Your emotional reactions may be even more apparent than your physical reactions to weaning. Much of your feeling about weaning will depend on your particular circumstances. If your baby is setting the pace for weaning, you may have the feeling that he is rejecting you. Rejoice, instead, in his push for independence and in his demonstration that he can take the initiative toward a new chapter in his life. This is only the first of many steps toward self-reliance that he will take in his lifetime. Your goal is to help him become as self-sufficient as possible, in small stages appropriate to his level of development.

While it can be a blow to realize that in one way your child does not need you as much as he did before, you should remember that he will need you even more in other ways. Right now, for example, he may particularly need the comfort of your arms and the reassurance of your love. Parenthood involves learning what a child needs at different stages in his life—and being able to give it.

Even if you yourself initiated the weaning process, you may be surprised to find that you feel more than a little sad

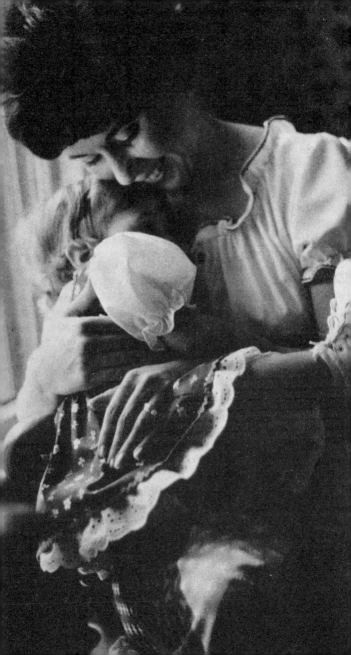

as nursing draws to a close. We all want our children to grow up, but then we have mixed feelings about our success. And so, the mother who leaves her youngster playing happily in the kindergarten room and the father who leads his daughter down the aisle as a bride feel a lump in the throat—even as they congratulate themselves for having helped their children to meet life's challenges with confidence and enthusiasm.

STAYING CLOSE WITH YOUR BABY

When you wean your baby and help him take this first big step toward independence, you will very likely tend to look back over his young life. You think of the nine months you carried him under your heart, nourishing him through your body, wondering who he was, what kind of a person he would be. You remember the exertion on both your parts as he burst into the world as an individual human being, breathing through his own lungs, making his own efforts to draw nourishment, learning how to cope with a strange world. You dwell on the time you spent together as a nursing couple, reliving the many happy moments you knew as you held your baby in your arms and gave to him of yourself.

And then you look forward. You think of the many other ways you will give of yourself to your child: the guidance you will provide to help him find himself, the unfailing love that will support him, the courage you will give him to let go of you and be his own person, the many happy hours you'll spend enjoying each other's company, playing together, having fun. You accept the fact that as a mother you will know tears and anger, as well as laughter and happiness. But just as you now remember, not the minor setbacks or worries about breastfeeding, but its heartfelt joys, so too with motherhood will you balance out its stresses with the love and the warmth that you gain from your relationship with your children.

SELECTED BIBLIOGRAPHY

BOOKS

Applebaum, R. M., M.D., *Abreast of the Times,* 1969

Bakwin, Harry, M.D. and Ruth M. Bakwin, M.D., *Clinical Management of Behavior Disorders in Children,* Phila.: W. B. Saunders, 1953

Berland, Theodore and Dr. Alfred E. Seyler, *Your Children's Teeth: a complete dental quide for parents,* New York: Meredith Press, 1968

Bradley, Robert A., *Husband-Coached Childbirth,* New York: Harper & Row, 1965

Brazelton, T. Berry, *Infants and Mothers: Differences in Development,* New York: Delacorte Press, 1969

Brecher, Edward M., *The Sex Researchers,* New York: New American Library, 1971

Chess, Stella, M.D., Alexander Thomas, M.D. and Herbert G. Birch, M.D., Ph.D., *Your Child is a Person,* New York: Parallax Publishing Co., 1965

Deutsch, Helene, *The Psychology of Women,* 2 vols., New York: Grune and Stratton, 1945

Flanagan, Geraldine Lux, *The First Nine Months of Life,* New York: Simon and Schuster, 1962

Folley, S. J., *The Physiology and Biochemistry of Lactation,* London: Oliver and Boyd, 1956

Gerard, Alice, *Please Breast-feed Your Baby,* New York: New American Library, 1971

Gray, Henry, F. R. S., *Anatomy of the Human Body,* 28th Edition. Philadelphia: Lea and Febiger, 1966

Guttmacher, Alan F., *Pregnancy and Birth: A Book for Expectant Parents,* New York: New American Library, 1962

Haire, Doris and John, *I. The Nurse's Contribution to Successful Breast-Feeding; II. The Medical Value of Breast-Feeding,* Bellevue, Wash.: International Childbirth Education Association, 1971

Hormann, Elizabeth, *Relactation: A Guide to Breastfeeding the Adopted Baby,* Belmont, Mass.: 1971

Jelliffe, Derrick B., *Infant Nutrition in the Tropics and Subtropics,* Geneva: World Health Organization, 1955

Kinsey, Alfred C. et al, *Sexual Behavior in the Human Female,* Philadelphia: W. B. Saunders Co., 1953

Kon, S. K. and A. T. Cowie, eds., *Milk: The Mammary Gland and Its Secretion*, 2 vols., New York: Academic Press, Inc., 1961

La Leche League International, *The Womanly Art of Breastfeeding*, Franklin Park, Illinois: La Leche League, 1958

Masters, William H., M.D. and Virginia E. Johnson, *Human Sexual Response*, Boston: Little, Brown, 1966

Mead, Margaret, *Male and Female*, New York: New American Library, 1955

Montagu, Ashley, *Life before Birth*, New York: New American Library, 1964

———, *Touching: The Human Significance of the Skin*, New York: Columbia University Press, 1971

Naish, F. Charlotte, M.D., *Breast Feeding: a guide to the natural feeding of infants*, London: Oxford University Press, 1948

Naismith, Grace, *Private and Personal*, New York: David McKay, 1966

Newton, Niles, *The Family Book of Child Care*, New York: Harper & Row, 1957

Newton, Niles, *Maternal Emotions*, New York: Paul B. Hoeber, Inc. (Harper & Row), 1955

Pryor, Karen, *Nursing Your Baby*, New York: Harper & Row, 1963

Ribble, Margaret A., M.D., *The Rights of Infants*, New York: Columbia University Press, 1965

Rugh, Roberts, Ph.D., Landrum B. Shettles, Ph.D., M.D. and Richard Einhorn, *From Conception to Birth: The Drama of Life's Beginnings*, New York: Harper & Row, 1971

Spock, Dr. Benjamin, *Baby and Child Care*, New York: Pocket Books, 1968

Stewart, Bernice C., M.S., *Best-Fed Babies*, Seattle, Wash.: Association for Childbirth Education, 1960, rev. 1965

Sulman, F. G., *Hypothalamic Control of Lactation*, Heidelberg: Springer-Verlag, 1970

Transcripts, Third Biennial Convention, Franklin Park, Ill.: La Leche League International, 1968

Waller, Harold, M.D., *The Breasts and Breast Feeding*, London: William Heinemann, 1957

What You Should Know about "the Pill," pamphlet prepared by the American Medical Association in cooperation with the American College of Obstetricians and Gynecologists, The Food and Drug Administration, and the Pharmaceutical Manufacturers Association. Chicago. Reviewed 1971.

ARTICLES

Anderson, Thomas A., Ph.D. and Samuel J. Fomon, M.D., "Commercially Prepared Strained and Junior Foods for Infants: Nutritional Considerations," in press, Journal of American Dietetic Association.

Applebaum, R. M., M.D., "The Modern Management of Successful Breast Feeding," Pediatric Clinics of North America, Vol. 17, No. 1, Feb. 1970, pp 203–225.

Arena, Jay M., M.D., "Contamination of the Ideal Food," Nutrition Today, Winter 1970, pp 2–8.

Bakwin, H., M.D., "Feeding Program for Infants," Federation Proceedings, 23: 66, 1964.

Baum, J. David, M.D., "Nutritional Value of Human Milk," Obstetrics-Gynecology, 37:.126–30, Jan. 1971.

Beal, Virginia A., M.P.H., "Breast- and Formula-Feeding of Infants," Journal of the American Dietetic Association, vol. 55, July 1969, pp 31–37.

Bernal, Judith and M. P. M. Richards, "The Effects of Bottle and Breast Feeding on Infant Development," Journal of Psychosomatic Research, 14: 247–252, Sept. 1970.

Borglin, Nils-Erik, M.D. and Lars-Erik Sandholm, M.D., "Effect of Oral Contraceptives on Lactation," Fertility-Sterility, 22: 39–41, Jan. 1971.

Brazelton, T. Berry, "Effect of Maternal Medication on the Neonate and his Behavior," Journal of Pediatrics, 58: 513–518, 1961.

"Breast Feeding and Antibodies," Infectious Diseases, April 15, 1971.

"Breast-milk Jaundice," British Medical Journal, 1:178, 25 July 1970.

Bullen, C. L. and A. T. Willis, "Resistance of the Breast-fed Infant to Gastroenteritis," Brit. Med. Jnl, 7 Aug. 1971, 3, 338–343.

Daniel, D. G., H. Campbell and A. C. Turnbull, "Puerperal Thromboembolism and Suppression of Lactation," Lancet, 2:287–289, 1967.

Devereux, W. P., M.D., "Management of Mastitis," American Journal of Obstetrics and Gynecology, 108: 78–81, Sept. 1970.

Eckstein, Herbert B. and Bridget Jack, "Breast-feeding and Anticoagulant Therapy," Lancet, 1:672, 1970.

"Errors in Babies' Food," Brit. Med. Jnl., 29 Nov. 1969, 515–516.

Filer, L. J., Jr., M.D., Ph.D., "Infant Feeding in the Nineteen Seventies," Pediatrics, 47:489–90, Mar. 1971.

Folley, S. J., D.Sc., F.R.S., "The Milk-ejection Reflex: a Neuroendocrine Theme in Biology, Myth and Art," Journal of Endocrinology, 44: x-xx, Aug. 1969.

Fomon, Samuel J., M.D., Lora N. Thomas, R.N. and L. J. Filer, Jr., M.D., Ph.D., "Acceptance of Unsalted Strained Foods by Normal Infants," Journal of Pediatrics, 76:242–246, Feb. 1970.

Fomon, Samuel J., M.D., L. J. Filer, Jr., M.D., Ph.D., Lora N. Thomas, R.N. and Ronald R. Rogers, B.S., "Growth and Serum Chemical Values of Normal Breastfed Infants," Acta Paediatrica Scandinavia, Supplement 202, 1970, pp 1–14.

Gartner, Lawrence M., M.D. and Irwin M. Arias, M.D., "Studies of Prolonged Neonatal Jaundice in the Breast-fed Infant," Journal of Pediatrics, 68:54–66, Jan. 1966.

Gioiosa, R., "Incidence of Pregnancy during Lactation in 500 Cases," American Journal of Obstetrics and Gynecology, 70:162, 1955.

Glaser, J. and D. E. Johnstone, "Prophylaxis of Allergic Disease in the Newborn," Jnl. Amer. Med. Assn, 153:620, 1953.

Goldstein, Marilyn, "Is No-Bra a No-No?", Newsday, Oct. 1, 1970.

Grantham-McGregor, S. M. and E. H. Back, "Breast Feeding in Kingston, Jamaica," Archives of Disease in Childhood, 45:404–9, June 1970.

Grulee, C. G. and H. N. Sanford, "The Influence of Breast and Artificial Feeding on Infantile Eczema," Journal of Pediatrics, 9:223, 1936.

Guthrie, Helen A., M.S. and George M. Guthrie, Ph.D., "The Resurgence of Natural Child Feeding: A Study of 129 Middle Class Mothers in a College Community," Clinical Pediatrics, Aug. 1966, vol. 5, no. 8, pp 481–484.

György, Paul, M.D., "Biochemical Aspects," in symposium "The Uniqueness of Human Milk," American Journal of Clinical Nutrition, Aug. 1971, pp 970–975.

——, "Protective Effects of Human Milk in Experimental Staphylococcal Infections," Science, 137:338, 1962.

Haagensen, C. D., "Breast Feeding and Breast Disease," Journal of the American Medical Women's Association, 20:956, 1965.

Harris, B. P., M.D., "Cancer of the Breast and Lactation," Canadian Medical Association Journal, 100:917, May 17, 1969.

Harris, Lloyd E., M.D., and James C. M. Chan, M.D., "Infant Feeding Practices," American Journal of Diseases of Children, 117:483–492, April 1969.

Hayward, John, "Hormones and Human Breast Cancer," Recent Results in Cancer Research, Springer-Verlag, New York.

Jeffcoate, T. N. A., Janine Miller, R. F. Roos and V. R. Tindall, "Puerperal Thromboembolism in Relation to the Inhibition of Lactation by Oestrogen Therapy," British Medical Journal, 4:19–25, 1968.

Jelliffe, Derrick B., M.D., F.R.C.P., "Breast-Milk and the World Protein Gap," Clinical Pediatrics, 7:96–99, Feb. 1968.

——, "Home Production of Protein (Breast Milk—A Neglected Infant Food)," Journal of Tropical Pediatrics, 15:31–33, 1969.

—— and E. F. Patrice Jelliffe, "Human Milk as an Ecological Force," delivered before First Asian Nutritional Congress, Hyderabad, India, 1971.

——, eds., "The Uniqueness of Human Milk," a symposium, American Journal of Clinical Nutrition, Aug. 1971, pp 968–1024.

Klackenberg, G. and I. Klackenberg-Larsson, "Development of Children in a Swedish Urban Community—Breast Feeding and Weaning—Social-Psychological Aspects," Acta Paediatrica Scandinavia (Supplement), 187:94–104, 1968.

Ladas, Alice K., Ed.D., "How to Help Mothers Breastfeed: Deductions from a Survey," Clinical Pediatrics, 9:702–5, Dec. 1970.

La Leche League News, bi-monthly newsletters, La Leche League International, Franklin Park, Ill.

MacKeith, Ronald, "Breast Feed for the First Two Months," Developmental Medicine and Child Neurology, 11:277–278, 1969.

McKigney, John I., "Economic Aspects," American Journal of Clinical Nutrition, Aug. 1971, pp 1005–1012.

MacMahon, Brian, T. M. Lin, C. R. Lowe et al, "Lactation and Cancer of the Breast. A Summary of an International Study," Bulletin of the World Health Organization, 42:185–94, 1970.

Mata, Leonardo J. and Richard G. Wyatt, "Host Resistance to Infection," American Journal of Clinical Nutrition, Aug. 1971, pp 976–986.

Matthews, T. S., "Infantile Gastroenteritis," British Medical Journal, 3:161, 18 July 1970.

Mendelsohn, Robert S., M.D., "Whom is the Hospital For?", paper read at Congress for Maternal and Infant Health, Chicago, Feb. 1963, reprinted in Child and Family, Oct. 1964.

Meyer, Herman F., M.D., "Breast Feeding in the United States: Extent and Possible Trend." Pediatrics, 22:115–121, July 1958.

———, "Breastfeeding in the United States: Report of a 1966 National Survey with Comparable 1946 and 1956 Data," Clinical Pediatrics, vol. 7, no. 12, Dec. 1968.

Moore, Dan H., Jesse Charney, Bernhard Kramarsky, Etienne Y. Lasfargues, Nurul H. Sarkar, Michael J. Brennan, John H. Burrows, Satyavati M. Sirsat, J. C. Paymaster and A. B. Vaidya, "Search for a Human Breast Cancer Virus," Nature, 229:611–614, Feb. 26, 1971.

"Mothers' Milk or Other Milk? (continued)," New York Times Magazine, July 4, 1971, p. 15. (Answers to article by William E. Homan, M.D., "Mothers' Milk or Other Milk?" in June 6, 1971 issue)

Newton, Michael, M.D., "Breast-Feeding by Adoptive Mother," Journal of American Medical Association, vol. 212, no. 11, June 15, 1970.

———, "Mammary Effects," American Journal of Clinical Nutrition, Aug. 1971, pp 987-990.

——— and Niles Newton, Ph.D., "The Normal Course and Management of Lactation," Clinical Obstetrics and Gynecology, 5:44–63, Mar. 1962.

Newton, Niles, Ph.D., Dudley Peeler, Ph.D. and Carolyn Rawlins, M.D., "Effect of Lactation on Maternal Behavior in Mice with Comparative Data on Humans," Lying-In: The Journal of Reproductive Medicine, 1:257–262, May–June 1968.

Newton, Niles, Ph.D., "Interrelationship between Various Aspects of the Female Reproductive Role: A Review," talk presented to annual meeting of American Psychopathological Association, New York, Feb. 5, 1971.

——— and Michael Newton, M.D., "Psychologic Aspects of Lactation," New England Journal of Medicine, 277:1179–1188, Nov. 30, 1967.

———, "Psychologic Differences between Breast and Bottle Feeding," American Journal of Clinical Nutrition, Aug. 1971, pp 993–1004.

"Recommended Dietary Allowances, Revised 1968," Dairy Council Digest, vol. 39, no. 6, Nov–Dec 1968.

Rossi, Alice S., "Maternalism, Sexuality and the New Feminism," paper presented to annual meeting of American Psychopathological Association, New York, Feb. 1971.

Salber, Eva J., M.D. and Manning Feinlib, M.D., "Breast-Feeding in Boston," Pediatrics, 37:299–303, Feb. 1966.

———, "The Unfashionable Practice of Breast Feeding," GP, 36: 128–131, Aug. 1967.

Schaefer, Otto, M.D., "Cancer of the Breast and Lactation," Canadian Medical Association Journal, 100:625–626, Apr. 5, 1969.

Smith, Beverly Bush, "Mother's Milk Saved Baby," Herald of Health, Jan. 1961, reprinted from Chicago Tribune.

Stevens, L. H., Ph.D., F.R.A.C.P., "The First Kilogram: 2. The Protein Content of Breast Milk of Mothers of Babies of Low Birth Weight," The Medical Journal of Australia, Sept. 13, 1969, pp 555–557.

Straub, Walter J., D.D.S., M.S., F.I.C.D., "Malfunction of the Tongue. Part I: The Abnormal Swallowing Habit: Its Cause, Effects and Results in Relation to Orthodontic Treatment and Speech Therapy," American Journal of Orthodontics, 46:404–424, June 1960.

Thoman, Evelyn B., Allan Wetzel and Seymour Levine, "Lactation Prevents Disruption of Temperature Regulation and Suppresses Adrenocortical Activity in Rats," Communications in Behavioral Biology, Part A,2, 165–171, Abstract No. 10680066 (1968).

———, R. L. Conner and Seymour Levine, "Lactation Suppresses Adrenal Corticosteroid Activity and Aggressiveness in Rats," Journal of Comparative and Physiological Psychology, 70:364–369, 1970.

Tompson, Marian, "The Convenience of Breastfeeding," American Journal of Clinical Nutrition, Aug. 1971, pp 991–992.

Vuorenkoski, V. et al, "The Effect of Cry Stimulus on the Temperature of the Lactating Breast of Primipara. A Thermographic Study.", Experientia, 25:1286–7, 15 Dec. 1969.

White, Mary, "Does Breast Feeding Space Babies?" dist. by La Leche League, reprinted from Marriage Magazine, St. Meinrad, Ind.

Whitley, N. N., "Breast Feeding the Premature," American Journal of Nursing, 70:1909, Sept. 1970.

Williams, Harold H., Ph.D., "Differences between Cow's and Human Milk," Jnl Amer. Med. Assn, 175:104–7, 14 Jan. 1961.

Winberg, J. and G. Wessner, "Does Breast Milk Protect Against Septicemia in the Newborn?" Lancet, 1:1091–1094, May 29, 1971.

INDEX

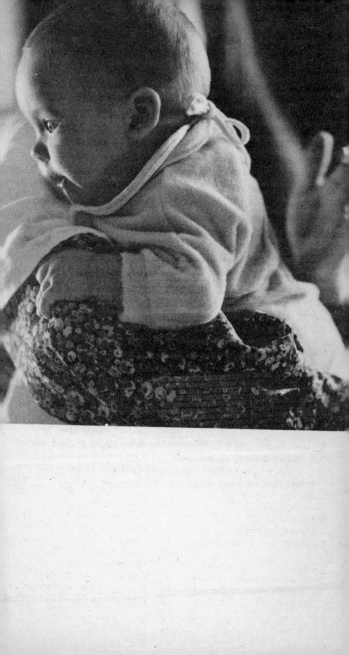

ABOUT THE AUTHORS

Marvin S. Eiger, M.D. is a leading pediatrician in New York's Greenwich Village and is a strong advocate of the natural way—over half the babies in his care are breastfed. Educated at Harvard University, Dr. Eiger received his medical training at New York University School of Medicine and served his residency in pediatrics at Bellevue Hospital. A Fellow of the American Academy of Pediatrics, Dr. Eiger is presently an attending pediatrician at the Beth Israel Medical Center and is an Associate Clinical Professor of Pediatrics at the Mount Sinai School of Medicine.

Sally Wendkos Olds is an award-winning author of nine books and over 200 articles that have appeared in major national magazines. She nursed her own three daughters and wrote her very first magazine article about breastfeeding when her oldest child was an infant. Her textbooks on human development have been read by over one million college students, and her most recent book is THE ETERNAL GARDEN: SEASONS OF OUR SEXUALITY. She lives on Long Island with her husband.